PERSONAL BANKRUPTCY

WHAT YOU SHOULD KNOW

Personal Bankruptcy

What You Should Know

ALICE GRIFFIN

THE CAKEWALK PRESS

Library of Congress Cataloging-in-Publication Data

Griffin, Alice E.
Personal Bankruptcy: What You Should Know / by Alice Griffin.
p. cm.
Includes index
1. Bankruptcy—United States—Popular Works.   I. Title.
KF1524.6.G75   1993   346.73'078   QBI93-834

ISBN 0-9636341-0-0   93-090301

Printed in the United States of America

10   9   8   7   6   5   4   3   2   1

For Mom and Kimmy

Acknowledgments

Many, many thanks to John Melissinos, Esq.; Luther Gatling, Budget and Credit Counseling Services, Inc., New York; Richardo Kilpatrick, Esq., Shermeta, Chimko and Kilpatrick, Rochester, Michigan; Isaac Blachor, Esq., Kroll & Blachor, Garden City, New York; the Honorable Cornelius Blackshear, United States Bankruptcy Judge, Southern District of New York. Writing this book would have been much more difficult without their help.

Warning and Disclaimer

This book is intended to provide information concerning the subject matters covered. It is sold with the understanding that the publisher and author are not engaged in rendering legal, accounting or other professional services. If legal or other expert assistance is necessary, the services of a competent professional should be sought.

This book describes the bankruptcy process as it applies to bankruptcy cases filed to eliminate consumer debts. It is not intended to advise anyone to file bankruptcy or to counsel anyone involved in a bankruptcy case.

Filing bankruptcy is a very serious step, and bankruptcy may not solve your financial problems because it does not eliminate all debts. *Anyone who has filed or who intends to file bankruptcy should contact a qualified bankruptcy lawyer for legal advice.*

Although many people file bankruptcy petitions on their own and represent themselves in bankruptcy cases, no one should base such a decision on information contained in this book. Bankruptcy contains many traps even for experienced bankruptcy lawyers, and a nonlawyer may do great harm by filing a bankruptcy petition on his or her own behalf or for someone else. The saying "When a person acts as his own lawyer he has a fool for a client" may be quite apt to a nonlawyer's venture into the complex world of bankruptcy law.

Every effort has been made to insure that the information contained in this book is accurate and complete. However, it is possible that it may contain typographical errors and, perhaps, errors in content as well. In any case, this book contains information about Title 11 of the United States Code and other laws that is accurate only up to the date this book was published.

The author has attempted to accurately state information concerning the subject matters covered. This book contains her interpretations of those subjects. She understands that others may disagree with her opinions and interpretations. *Neither the author nor the publisher shall be liable for losses or damages, actual or consequential, resulting or allegedly resulting, from the contents of this book.*

Contents

x

Introduction

What does it mean to "file" bankruptcy? A person files bankruptcy when he asks a United States Bankruptcy Court to grant him the protection of the federal bankruptcy laws.

The decision to file bankruptcy is often painful. Usually it is made when a person can no longer bear the annoyance of creditors' telephone calls and letters demanding debt payments, or when creditors sue to attach property or garnish wages. Every year such pressures compel hundreds of thousands of Americans to seek debt relief in the nation's bankruptcy courts.

Often people who file bankruptcy are stereotyped as irresponsible deadbeats who run up credit card debt and then file bankruptcy to get out from under. Although many people do file bankruptcy because of excessive credit card use, most people who are forced to seek bankruptcy protection do so because of an unexpected financial problem such as a sudden loss of employment or income, or medical bills not covered by insurance. Consumer bankruptcies skyrocketed in the late 1980s and early 1990s due to the nation's severe recession and weak economy. These hard times left many people who had previously enjoyed sterling credit ratings jobless and unable to pay their debts.

If you're like most people who file bankruptcy, you know very little about the bankruptcy process, and will wait until the eve of foreclosure or until after your pay has been garnished to file.

Ignorance of the bankruptcy process or filing bankruptcy hastily can have disastrous effects on your bankruptcy case. If you are ignorant of the bankruptcy process, you will not know how to prepare for bankruptcy, and, if you file with no advance planning, you may not be able to get the most out of bankruptcy and may run the risk of filing too late to save your property.

If you wait until the last minute to file bankruptcy, you also increase the chance that you'll be so desperate for bankruptcy counsel that you'll hire the first lawyer you find. Since your bankruptcy is one of the most important legal events in your life, using the first lawyer you find without regard to that lawyer's experience and qualifications invites disaster. Even an experienced bankruptcy lawyer needs time to plan strategy and advise you of any prebankruptcy acts you should perform. By waiting until the last minute to file your bankruptcy case you may seriously handicap your lawyer and limit his usefulness to you.

There is no reason for you to have these problems. Your bankruptcy case should proceed as smoothly as possible. I've written a book that I believe will help you by providing you with useful information about the bankruptcy process. Among other things, it tells you:

- what bankruptcy can do for you;
- what to expect when in bankruptcy;
- the consequences of bankruptcy;
- how to find a competent bankruptcy lawyer;
- some of the rules governing your relationship with your bankruptcy lawyer; and
- what kinds of conduct before and during a bankruptcy case can get you into trouble.

It also describes alternatives to bankruptcy that may allow you to obtain the benefits of bankruptcy without further damaging your credit rating.

If you understand the bankruptcy process, you will be better equipped to face one of the most significant legal events in your life, and you may be able to save more of your property from your creditors.

GOOD LUCK!

Alice Griffin
1994

CHAPTER ONE

Bankruptcy Relief Available to You as a Consumer Debtor

Debts for your personal needs are called consumer debts. If you file bankruptcy to rid yourself of consumer debts, your bankruptcy will be a consumer bankruptcy and you will be a debtor. (Consumer bankruptcy is entirely different from business bankruptcy. In a business bankruptcy, the debtor is a business or an individual involved in business, and the debts are for business purposes.)

Most people who seek bankruptcy protection do so under Chapter 7 or 13 of Title 11 of the United States Code. Title 11 of the United States Code is informally called the "Bankruptcy Code." The Bankruptcy Code is federal law and overrides many aspects of state laws including those that would require you to pay certain debts.

The fundamental purpose of bankruptcy is to help people obtain a fresh financial start without burdensome debts. The Bankruptcy Code contains three mechanisms to further this purpose:

(1) the *automatic stay*—an injunction that protects debtors and their property from creditors;

(2) *exemptions*—which allow debtors to keep some property from creditors; and

(3) *discharge*—which cancels certain types of consumer debts.

Chapter 7: Liquidation Bankruptcy

Chapter 7 of the Bankruptcy Code is the portion of the Code providing for *liquidation*: distribution of a person's nonexempt property to that person's creditors. Most people who need relief from consumer debts file under Chapter 7. Chapter 7 may be right for you if you have little property and are not concerned with saving a large asset—such as a house—from creditors.

Filing under Chapter 7 does not mean you lose your property. On the contrary, by filing bankruptcy you will place some (and possibly all) of your property beyond the reach of your creditors. This property will be "exempt." The remainder of your property will go to satisfy the claims of your creditors. If you're like most people who file under Chapter 7, you will have little or no nonexempt property, and your creditors will get nothing from you.

Chapter 13: Wage Earner Bankruptcy

Chapter 13 may be right for you if you have steady employment and wish to keep a valuable asset, such as your home. Chapter 13 allows you to create a "plan" to pay your creditors over time—usually three to five years.

EXAMPLE
John is behind in his mortgage payments and the bank threatens foreclosure. His past due mortgage payments total $10,000. John files Chapter 13 bankruptcy. He creates a plan to pay the bank the $10,000 over a three-year period at 10% interest. (The interest compensates the bank for having to wait for its money.) In addition to making his plan payments, John must make his regular monthly mortgage payments.

If you have unsecured debts (debts for which none of your property is collateral) that total less than $100,000 and secured debts (*see Chapter Three*) totalling less than $350,000, you can file Chapter 13 bankruptcy. A person with a $375,000 mortgage (a secured debt) would be ineligible for Chapter 13 protection.

There are significant benefits to filing under Chapter 13. First, you may be able to keep valuable assets that you would probably lose in Chapter 7. (Most Chapter 13 debtors are home owners who want to avoid foreclosure.) Second, Chapter 13 allows you to eliminate certain debts that cannot be eliminated in Chapter 7.

Sometimes a case filed under Chapter 13 is converted by the bankruptcy court to a Chapter 7 liquidation bankruptcy. This happens when: (1) the bankruptcy judge won't approve the debtor's plan; or (2) the debtor cannot pay the debts in accordance with the plan.

Because Chapter 13 probably offers you more than Chapter 7, you will want to work hard to avoid having your Chapter 13 case converted to Chapter 7. However, if your Chapter 13 case must be converted to a Chapter 7 case through no fault of your own, and you have already paid as much to your creditors as they would have received if you had originally filed under Chapter 7 (which in most consumer cases is nothing), the bankruptcy court may grant you the more generous Chapter 13 discharge even though your case is converted to Chapter 7.

Other Types of Bankruptcy Relief

■ Chapter 11: Business Bankruptcy

Although this book describes only Chapter 7 and Chapter 13 bankruptcies, there are two other types of bankruptcy relief available for people in financial distress. Chapter 11 is for businesses, people in business, or people who have assets valued higher than the limits assigned in Chapter 13.

Chapter 11 is complicated. If you are a business person in financial distress, you should find a good Chapter 11 lawyer—fast. Ask your present attorney for a referral. You can also ask your state and local bar associations to recommend experienced Chapter 11 lawyers.

Many people assume every lawyer can handle any legal task, and ask the lawyer they use for general legal matters to handle their Chapter 11 case. This is often a disastrous mistake. Bankruptcy is a specialty. If your business is in trouble, you need advice from a good Chapter 11 lawyer. Look at it this way—if you learned you had cancer, would you ask your general practice doctor to treat you? Of course not. Your life would be at stake and you would try to locate the best cancer specialist you could afford. The same principle applies to business bankruptcy problems.

It is very difficult to reorganize a business in bankruptcy. Most reorganization attempts fail. For your troubled business— your livelihood—to have a real chance at survival, get yourself the best Chapter 11 lawyer you can afford.

■ Chapter 12: Family Farmer Bankruptcy

Chapter 12 provides bankruptcy relief for family farmers. Chapter 12 is perhaps the most specialized area of bankruptcy. I am a bankruptcy lawyer yet I know almost nothing about Chapter 12. Don't be shocked. Would you expect a cardiologist to be able to perform brain surgery? If you need a Chapter 12 lawyer, call your bankruptcy court and ask for the number of the United States Trustee. Then call the United States Trustee and ask for the names of the local Chapter 12 trustees. (Chapter 12 trustees oversee Chapter 12 cases.) Call the trustees and ask for referrals.

CHAPTER TWO

How Bankruptcy Helps and Hurts You

Bankruptcy can provide you with three extraordinary benefits:

- *The Automatic Stay*—Stops all debt collection activity;

- *Exemptions*—Allow you to place some of your property beyond your creditors' reach; and

- *Discharge of Your Debts*—Eliminates your "dischargeable" debts.

These benefits are not without a price: bankruptcy is the worst mark you can have in your credit history, and it will remain in your credit file for at least ten years.

Benefits of Bankruptcy

■ The Automatic Stay: Your Shield Against Creditors

You've probably heard someone say something like: "If you're in bankruptcy, your creditors can't touch you." Such statements refer to the *automatic stay*. The automatic stay prevents creditors from any attempts to collect debts from you, and it becomes effective the minute you file bankruptcy.

What the Automatic Stay Prohibits

- **Collection efforts** (including oral or written demands for payment) against you or your property.

EXAMPLE
Joan owes Burke's department store $2,500 on her Burke's store account and she is past due on her payments. Burke's collections department regularly calls Joan at home and work demanding payment. Joan files Chapter 7 bankruptcy. Burke's can no longer demand payment from her.

- **Commencement or continuation of legal or other action against you or your property.**

EXAMPLE

The American Credit Card Company sued Mark for $10,000. Mark files Chapter 7 bankruptcy. The lawsuit is stopped by the automatic stay.

- **Any attempt to exercise control over your property including asset seizure, attachment, levy, foreclosure, or garnishment.** The automatic stay is a federal injunction that prevents state and federal agencies (including the Internal Revenue Service) from committing the acts listed above.

EXAMPLE

ABC Bank has foreclosed on James's house. James is ten months behind in his mortgage payments for a total of $10,000. The foreclosure sale is scheduled for Friday at noon. On Friday at 11:00 A.M., James files Chapter 13 bankruptcy. At 11:15 A.M., James calls ABC Bank and reports that he has filed bankruptcy. The foreclosure sale must be cancelled.

Evictions, most family court proceedings, and administrative proceedings are other examples of legal actions stopped by the automatic stay. For example, if you are being sued for divorce by your spouse when you file bankruptcy, the divorce proceeding is stopped by the automatic stay. (Divorce actions are halted because they usually involve property or support awards.)

Many people want to know if bankruptcy protects loan co-signers and guarantors. *Chapter 13* bankruptcy does protect co-signers and guarantors of consumer debts. This protection ends, however, if your Chapter 13 case is:

- dismissed (the bankruptcy court refuses to give you the protection of the Bankruptcy Code);
- closed (your bankruptcy case ends); or
- converted to Chapter 7.

What the Automatic Stay Does Not Prohibit

- **Criminal actions or proceedings against you**
- **Collection of alimony, maintenance, or support obligations.** You may be required to continue making alimony, maintenance, or support payments.
- **Exercise of police powers.** Governmental units (police, FBI, National Guard, etc.) may prevent or stop you from committing fraud, or violating environmental protection, consumer protection, safety, or similar police or regulatory laws.
- **Enforcement of nonmonetary judgments in exercise of police powers.** A governmental unit may enforce a judgment against you that doesn't include a fine. For example, you could be sent to jail for driving under the influence of drugs or alcohol although you are in bankruptcy.

Violations of the Automatic Stay

If a creditor or other person violates the automatic stay, you can sue him. I have seen debtors sue their creditors for violating the automatic stay—and win. Generally speaking, fines in such cases are nominal; however, in some cases where a creditor's violation of the stay was malicious or willful, bankruptcy courts have awarded punitive damages.

EXAMPLE
Sam owes money to ABC Bank for his ABC credit card. ABC Bank calls Sam to request payment after Sam has filed his bankruptcy petition. ABC Bank has violated the automatic stay. Sam can sue ABC Bank for violating the automatic stay. If Sam shows that ABC Bank acted willfully, he may recover actual damages, including attorneys' fees and costs, and, perhaps, may recover punitive damages also.

Creditors can request that the bankruptcy court "lift" the automatic stay to permit them to perform acts otherwise prohibited by the automatic stay. They make this request by filing a "motion to lift the automatic stay." If a creditor has any doubts about whether the automatic stay prohibits him from acting against a debtor or the debtor's property, the creditor should obtain relief from the automatic stay rather than risk violating it.

■ Exemptions

Bankruptcy is designed to give you a fresh start by eliminating your debts and protecting you from your creditors. Because you need basic necessities for your fresh start, the Bankruptcy Code allows you to "exempt" property, that is, to put certain property out of your creditors' reach.

The Bankruptcy Code contains exemptions you can use *unless your state's law provides otherwise.* Some states have their own exemptions and restrict their residents to the state exemptions. This may not be a bad thing since many states offer exemptions that are more generous than those in the Bankruptcy Code.

The Bankruptcy Code Exemptions

The Bankruptcy Code provides the following exemptions:

- **Homestead**—$7,500 maximum value ("home" includes a co-op, condominium, or trailer);
- **Automobile**—$1,200 maximum value;
- **Furniture, Household Goods, Clothing, Appliances, Books, Animals, Crops, or Musical Instruments**—$4,000 maximum value, and not more than $200 for any one item;
- **Jewelry**—$500 maximum value;
- **Any Property** (this is called the "wildcard" exemption)—$400 plus up to $3,750 of any unused portion of your *home* exemption;
- **Tools of your trade** (items you or a dependent need in connection with a trade or business)—$750 maximum value;
- **Unmatured life insurance policies;**
- **Dividends, interest, or loan value of a life insurance policy**—$4,000 maximum;
- **Doctor prescribed health aids;**
- **Social security, unemployment compensation, or public assistance;**
- **Veterans' benefits;**
- **Disability or sickness benefits;**

- **Alimony, support, or maintenance** to the extent necessary to support you or your dependent;
- **Stock bonus, pension, profit-sharing, annuity, or similar plans**—to the extent reasonably necessary to support you or your dependent;
- **Personal injury recoveries** (for bodily injury only—not pain and suffering)—up to $7,500;
- **Wrongful death benefits** to the extent necessary to support you or your dependent;
- **Crime victim's restitution payments;**
- **Life insurance payments** to the extent necessary to support you or your dependent.

Exemptions with dollar limits are doubled if you file bankruptcy with your spouse.

State Law Exemptions

Once again: *The Bankruptcy Code exemptions may not be available to you.* The Bankruptcy Code says that your state may restrict you to your state's exemptions, if any. If your state has decided to restrict its residents to its own exemptions, you are limited to using your state's exemptions. For example, New York residents are limited to New York's exemptions—although they may also use any federal non-Bankruptcy Code exemptions to which they are entitled.

On the other hand, your state may give you a choice between your state exemptions and the Bankruptcy Code exemptions. If your state does this, you may use either the Bankruptcy Code's exemptions or your state's exemptions (plus any exemptions available under other federal law).

If you can choose between the Bankruptcy Code exemptions and your state's exemptions, you should compare them closely, because there may be a significant difference between the exemptions in the two plans. For example, some states, such as Florida and Texas, have extremely generous homestead exemptions. (It is not uncommon for a resident of another state who expects to file bankruptcy to sell her property, move to Florida or Texas, and buy a home there with the proceeds.) Some states, like New Jersey and Connecticut, have no homestead exemption. You should discuss at length your exemptions options with your bankruptcy lawyer to insure that you retain as much of your property as possible after bankruptcy.

At the time of this writing, the following states permit their residents to choose between the Bankruptcy Code and state exemptions: Arkansas, Connecticut, District of Columbia, Hawaii, Massachusetts, Michigan, Minnesota, New Mexico, New Jersey, Pennsylvania, Puerto Rico, Rhode Island, South Carolina, Texas, Vermont, Virgin Islands, Washington, and Wisconsin.

Residents of these states are restricted to their state's exemptions and any applicable federal non-Bankruptcy Code exemptions: Alabama, Alaska, Arizona, California, Colorado, Delaware, Florida, Georgia, Idaho, Illinois, Indiana, Iowa, Kansas, Kentucky, Louisiana, Maine, Maryland, Mississippi, Missouri, Montana, Nebraska, Nevada, New Hampshire, New York, North Carolina, North Dakota, Ohio, Oklahoma, Oregon, South Dakota, Tennessee, Utah, Virginia, West Virginia, and Wyoming.

There are two ways to obtain up-do-date information about your state's exemptions law: ask your lawyer or obtain *How to File Bankruptcy* (Nolo Press, 950 Parker St., Berkeley, CA 94710-9867, toll free number 1-800-992-6656).

Objections to Exemptions

Your creditors or your bankruptcy trustee (the court official overseeing your case—to be discussed later) may object to your exemptions. The most common reasons for an exemption challenge are:

- **Misclassification**. The property you claim as exempt does not fit within the category to which you assigned it.

EXAMPLE
You are a truck driver and you want to exempt your truck as a tool of your trade rather than as an automobile.

- **Incorrect value.** The value of your interest in property you have listed as exempt exceeds the exemption limit.

EXAMPLE
You claim a bracelet worth $2,000 under the jewelry exemption. Your trustee objects on the grounds that its value exceeds the exemption limit.

You may decide to settle an exemptions objection by reaching a compromise or paying your trustee the value of the property. Your decision depends on the importance of the property at issue. Whether it is possible for you to fight an objection to an exemption will depend on your retainer agreement with your lawyer and your financial resources. (Many lawyer retainer agreements specify that the lawyer will do no more for you than file the papers needed to start a bankruptcy case.)

Waiving Your Exemptions

You may decide to waive your exemptions. Why would you want to do this? Well, you might want to make more of your property available to your creditors. Again, why? You might feel a moral obligation to pay your creditors, or you might feel that your standing in the community would improve if you give your creditors more property. Chances are you won't feel this way if you live in a big city where you never see your creditors. However, if you live in a small town and your creditors sit next to you in church or their children attend school with yours, you may want to pay them more to retain their good will.

If you do waive your exemptions, you may still keep certain property from creditors:

- **Any exempt property that is subject to a creditor's judicial lien.** If a creditor used a judgment obtained against you to put a lien on your property, that creditor has a "judicial lien" on your property.

- **Personal property that is collateral for a debt.** If a creditor lent you money and took any of the following property as collateral, you can eliminate the creditor's lien on the property: furniture, household goods, clothing, appliances, books, animals, crops, musical instruments, jewelry, tools of your trade, or doctor prescribed health aids.

How Exemptions Are Calculated

An important point to know about exemptions: They are deducted from your *equity* in specific property. Equity is the value in property that remains after your creditors' interests are deducted.

Equity = Value of Property Minus Creditors' Interests

and

The Value of an Exemption Is Less Than or Equal to Equity

EXAMPLE

If your house is valued at $300,000 and is subject to mortgages and tax liens totalling $250,000, you have $50,000 equity. If you claimed equity in your home as exempt, you could exempt part or all (depending on the applicable exemption limit) of the $50,000.

Because exemptions are so important, valuation of property is also important. Who puts a value on your house? Answer: an appraiser. Your mortgage holder will hire its own appraiser. Most likely its appraiser will not agree with your appraiser's judgment as to the value of your property: the mortgage holder will want to argue that you have no equity in the property. (If you have no equity in the property, the creditor would have grounds for relief from the automatic stay. (*See "Property in Which You Have No Equity" on the following page.)*

If the property at issue is a car, who assigns value? Most bankruptcy judges recognize well-known used car appraisal guides such as the *Kelley Blue Book* as authoritative on the value of a used car. However, such guides are not necessarily the last word, and sometimes debtors successfully challenge their valuations of cars.

Property In Which You Have No Equity

If your property has no equity from which you can claim an exemption (for example, your home is worth $100,000 but is subject to a $130,000 mortgage), generally speaking, one of three things will happen: (1) the creditor(s) will ask the bankruptcy judge to "lift" the automatic stay, which would permit him to take the property; (2) your Chapter 7 or 13 trustee will "abandon" the property (give it to the creditor); or (3) you will pay off some or all of the debts on the property.

In most cases, creditors won't wait for the trustee to abandon the property, but will seek relief from the automatic stay. Sometimes, a debtor will pay off some or all of the liens securing his property. (Paying down liens on property before filing bankruptcy is a common prebankruptcy planning maneuver. *See "Prebankruptcy Planning" below.*)

Prebankruptcy Planning

To get the most out of bankruptcy, you must prepare *before* you file. This is called *prebankruptcy planning*. Prebankruptcy planning means arranging (or rearranging) your property to allow you to take maximum advantage of available exemptions. Prebankruptcy planning often includes converting nonexempt assets into exempt ones.

Failure to adequately prepare for your bankruptcy case could mean losing property like a home in spite of generous exemption laws. For example, some states, like Montana, require homeowners to declare that they will file homestead exemptions before they file bankruptcy. If you fail to comply with such a requirement, you may not be able to exempt your home from your creditors' reach after you file bankruptcy.

Once again: *Consult a qualified bankruptcy lawyer before you file bankruptcy.*

■ Discharge: Your Release from Burdensome Debts

A fundamental goal of bankruptcy is to give you a "fresh start" without burdensome debts. The purpose of bankruptcy is to free you from the debts that drove you into bankruptcy. A discharge releases you from liability for the discharged debts and prohibits your creditors from ever taking any action against you to collect those debts.

Your discharge also stops your creditors from:

- making any communication regarding the debt with you, your relatives, employees, or friends, including telephone calls, letters, and personal contact;

and

- taking action against your property to collect a discharged debt.

EXAMPLE

Mary owes Simms, Robinson & Co. $5,000 for charges she made on her Simms, Robinson charge card. Mary files Chapter 7 bankruptcy. The bankruptcy court grants Mary a discharge of the Simms, Robinson debt. Simms, Robinson can never try to collect the debt from Mary or her property, and the debt is wiped out.

In 1992, a debtor in Ohio sued a creditor who tried to collect a discharged debt, and was awarded a total of $22,398.87. Fifteen thousand of that was awarded as punitive damages.

A discharge extinguishes "dischargeable" debts only. If a particular debt is nondischargeable, it survives bankruptcy and the creditor who is owed the debt may try to collect the debt from you or your property after you are out of bankruptcy (after your case is closed). Dischargeable and nondischargeable debts are discussed at length in Chapter Four.

If you file under Chapter 7, you will probably receive a discharge within 120 days after you file your petition. However, discharge plays a different role in Chapter 13 cases. In Chapter 13 you will receive a discharge from dischargeable debts after you complete all payments under your Chapter 13 plan.

EXAMPLE

John is $10,000 behind on his mortgage payments. Also, he owes ABC Bank $5,000 on his ABC credit card. To save his home from foreclosure, John files Chapter 13 bankruptcy. The bankruptcy court approves John's plan to pay the $10,000 mortgage debt over three years, and the discharge of the the ABC debt when the plan is paid in full. When John has made all his plan payments, the ABC debt will be discharged.

Chapter 13 allows you to discharge certain debts that are not dischargeable in Chapter 7. The scope of the Chapter 13 discharge is discussed in Chapter Four.

■ Other Benefits of Bankruptcy

Chapter 13 and Executory Contracts

Don't be intimidated by the fancy term "executory." What is an executory contract? A contract or lease is *executory* if both parties to the agreement have duties to perform under it. For example, most states say that under an apartment lease, a tenant has a duty to pay rent, and a landlord has a duty to protect the tenant's right to enjoy the apartment in peace. A rental lease, while in force, is executory because both parties, landlord and tenant, have duties to perform under the lease. Once the lease is terminated, however, it is no longer executory because both parties no longer have duties.

Bankruptcy allows you to "assume" (keep) or "reject" (eliminate) an executory contract or lease. This is a great benefit for you because you, like many people, may be a party to a lease or contract you can't afford to honor. For example, you may have a long lease on an apartment or house at a rent that is way above market rates, or you may be locked into some other type of burdensome lease or contract. Chapter 13 bankruptcy allows you to *reject* the burdensome lease. (Chapter 7 does also, but the Chapter 7 trustee must make the request.)

What kinds of leases and contracts are affected? All kinds: real property leases, automobile leases, layaways, contingent fee arrangements with lawyers, rent-to-own agreements, installment contracts, etc.

If you reject a contract or lease, the other party will have a claim against you, but the claim will probably be dischargeable.

On the other hand, you may be a party to a valuable lease or contract that you want to keep or renew. Bankruptcy allows you to do this also by *assuming* the lease or contract.

To assume a lease or contract you must either make up all the past due payments you owe—this is known as "curing defaults"; or give the other party prompt assurance that you will pay what you owe in the near future.

EXAMPLE

Joe, a Chapter 13 debtor, leases his car from Sam's Car Land. Joe wants to keep the car although he is three months behind in his lease payments. Sam's Car Land files a motion to lift the automatic stay to recover the car and terminate the lease. If Joe wants to keep the car, he must either pay the past due lease payments or give Sam's Car Land adequate assurance that he will pay the past due amounts promptly.

If you decide to reject a contract or lease, your attorney will take the appropriate steps. If you reject an executory contract or lease, the other party has a claim against you for any damages they will suffer as a result of the rejection. (Also, if it is an installment contract, you will have to return the property you were paying for within a reasonable time.) Although the claim arises after bankruptcy, it is treated as though it arose before you filed bankruptcy. (This is so because if the claim for damages were treated as though it arose after bankruptcy, you wouldn't be able to discharge it.)

Here is another point you should know about executory contracts: Sometimes a creditor will attempt to cancel a lease or contract merely because a debtor has filed bankruptcy. The creditor will point to a provision in the lease or contract that says it can be terminated because you are in bankruptcy. Such provisions are invalid. Although the creditor has the right to refuse to enter into a *new* lease or contract with you, if the lease or contract gives you the right to renew at your option, you may do so.

Continuation of Your Utility Services

Many debtors are behind in their utility (gas, electricity, telephone) payments when they file bankruptcy. A utility may not discontinue, alter, or refuse service to you because you filed bankruptcy.

However, a utility may discontinue, alter, or refuse service if, within 20 days after you file bankruptcy, you do not give them a deposit or other form of security to assure future payment.

Reinstatement of a Suspended Driver's License

If your driver's license was suspended *because of your failure to pay traffic fines*, the licensing authority must reinstate your license when those fines are discharged in bankruptcy. If your license was suspended for some other reason, bankruptcy may not help you recover driving privileges.

Release of Student Transcripts

If you owed a *public* school money for student loans and the school withheld your transcript because of your failure to pay the loans, the school must release your transcript if the loans are discharged in your bankruptcy.

Disadvantages of Bankruptcy

■ Damage to Your Credit Rating

A notation that you have filed bankruptcy will remain in your credit file for *at least ten years*. THIS IS TRUE EVEN IF FOR SOME REASON YOUR DEBTS ARE NOT DISCHARGED. (*See Chapter Four for information on discharge.*) During this time you will find it extremely difficult to obtain credit or anything else that requires a review of your credit report. (For example, renting an apartment or a house may be difficult since many landlords require credit reports from prospective tenants.)

Obtaining a Mortgage after Bankruptcy

It will probably be impossible for you to obtain a mortgage. Although mortgages are secured debts and are, therefore, less risky for lenders than unsecured loans, a bankruptcy in your past will scare banks because they'll assume you present a foreclosure risk. Banks hate foreclosures, so it's unlikely that a bank will give you a mortgage on standard terms after bankruptcy. You might be able to obtain one if you offer a bank a very large down payment and extra mortgage interest to cover the increased risk of foreclosure.

Obtaining Credit Cards after Bankruptcy

You may be able to obtain credit cards after bankruptcy. Many people who have been through bankruptcy find that the creditors to whom they owed money for credit card debt send them new credit cards after bankruptcy!

Why would a creditor issue a new credit card to you after you discharged the debts you owed? Because you're probably a better credit risk after bankruptcy! Again, why? Because of the "six year bar." After bankruptcy you can't get a Chapter 7 discharge for six years (unless your bankruptcy case was a Chapter 13 and you gave your unsecured creditors at least 70% of what you owed them). And you are no longer burdened by the old debts that drove you into bankruptcy—which means you'll have money to pay new debts!

If you can't get new credit cards from your old credit card issuers, you may be able to obtain a "secured" credit card—a credit card secured by a cash deposit. This means that you deposit cash with the credit card issuer and make "charges" against this cash deposit. For a list of banks offering secured credit cards, see Appendix D.

Anti-discrimination Protection

The Bankruptcy Code provides you with some protection against discrimination after your bankruptcy. *Governmental units* (including states, cities, and their agencies) may not discriminate against you because you filed bankruptcy, obtained a discharge, *or* were associated with someone who filed bankruptcy (such as a spouse). Discrimination by governmental units includes denying, revoking, suspending, or refusing to renew a license, permit, charter, franchise; and denying or terminating employment.

In spite of this protection, at least one person who has filed bankruptcy has been denied a license by a state agency. A man who filed bankruptcy was denied admission to the New York bar. The court reviewing the applicant's appeal from the denial said that he wasn't denied admission to the bar because he'd filed bankruptcy, but because his bankruptcy was a sign of financial irresponsibility.

Private employers are prohibited from denying or terminating employment because you filed bankruptcy, obtained a discharge, or were associated with someone who filed bankruptcy. Some employers now require credit reports from prospective employees. If a prospective employer denies you employment because you filed bankruptcy, she certainly won't tell you, and it may be very difficult for you to prove discrimination.

Let's face it—in our society, credit and creditworthiness are basic necessities, and ten years is a long time for you to do without them. On the other hand, so many people have filed bankruptcy that you may find that some of the people you'll ask for credit after bankruptcy have filed bankruptcy themselves!

Chapter Three

The Bankruptcy Process

To obtain bankruptcy protection, you must file a *bankruptcy petition*. A bankruptcy petition is a formal request for the protection of the bankruptcy laws. There is an Official Form for bankruptcy petitions. A copy is contained in Appendix A. When you file a bankruptcy petition, you become a debtor.

Eligibility

Before you file a bankruptcy petition, you must make sure that you are eligible to "become a debtor." You may become a debtor if *both* of these conditions are true:

(1) You reside or have a home, a place of business, or property in the United States.

(2) Within the past 180 days, you have not been a debtor in another bankruptcy case that was dismissed because:

   • you willfully failed to abide by bankruptcy court orders;

   • you failed to appear before the bankruptcy court to properly prosecute that bankruptcy case; or

   • you requested that the case be dismissed after a creditor made a motion to lift the automatic stay.

Any American citizen living in the United States or its territories or possessions (including Puerto Rico) can satisfy requirement (1). If you are a non-U.S. citizen you can do the same if you live, have a home in, have a place of business in, or have property in, the United States, unless some other law prohibits you from filing a bankruptcy petition. Requirement (1) is intended to insure that persons seeking bankruptcy protection in the United States have a sufficient link to the United States to invoke the protection of its bankruptcy laws.

Requirement (2) is intended to prevent "serial bankruptcy filings" by people who do not intend to follow through with the process but merely want temporary reprieves from their creditors. If you were a debtor within the last 180 days, and your bankruptcy case was dismissed for one of the reasons listed in requirement (2), then you may not file bankruptcy now.

Talk to your bankruptcy lawyer about this. You probably will learn that you must wait to file until 180 days from the date your last bankruptcy case was dismissed.

Mechanics of Filing Bankruptcy

■ Where You File Your Bankruptcy Petition

Bankruptcy courts are federal courts, and they are located throughout the nation in various "districts." Each state has at least one district. Some states, like California and Texas, have several districts.

You must file your bankruptcy petition with the United States Bankruptcy Court located in the district where your home, residence, principal place of business, or principal assets have been for at least the 180 days immediately preceding the date the bankruptcy petition is filed.

For example, if you have lived in Los Angeles for the past 180 days, you would file your bankruptcy petition in the United States Bankruptcy Court, Central District of California. It would not be proper for you to file your petition in San Francisco, which is located in the Northern District of California.

Sometimes a debtor has a choice about where to file a petition. If you have a choice, your lawyer may suggest one district over another because treatment of debtors by bankruptcy courts can vary widely from district to district.

■ Married Couples Filing Jointly

Many people file joint petitions with their spouses. They do this for several reasons. First, because many spouses are jointly liable for problem debts, unless both file bankruptcy, the non-filing spouse will be subject to creditor demands (except in Chapter 13 cases if the spouse is a co-signer or guarantor and the debt is a consumer debt). Second, joint petitions usually allow couples to exempt twice as much property from creditors. Third, spouses can file jointly for the cost of a single fee.

In some cases it's not a good idea for spouses to file jointly. For example, in a situation where one spouse owes all the debts and the other spouse is not responsible for them, there might be no need for both to file.

Other considerations, such as whether a couple lives in a community property state, may be relevant to the decision to file a joint petition.

■ Schedules

When you file a bankruptcy petition you must give the bankruptcy court lists of your assets, creditors, liabilities and other information concerning your financial affairs. These lists are called *schedules* and must be filed with the court in the proper form within 15 days from the date you file your petition unless you receive permission from the bankruptcy court to file them later. (*The forms for bankruptcy schedules are included in Appendix A.*) If you do not file your schedules within 15 days, your case may be dismissed. You must list property claimed as exempt on the appropriate schedule form. Whether specific property may be claimed as exempt depends upon whether you are entitled to your state's or the Bankruptcy Code's exemption provisions.

Also, you must list *all* your creditors on your schedules. If you don't, the debts owed to the omitted creditors may not be discharged.

■ Meeting of Creditors

After your petition and schedules are filed, a date will be set for you to appear before your creditors so that they can question you about your debts and your property. This meeting is informally called a "341 meeting" because Section 341 of the Bankruptcy Code requires it. Your creditors probably won't appear at your 341 meeting because they forfeit no rights by not attending.

■ Chapter 7 and 13 Trustees

After you file your petition, a *trustee* will be appointed to oversee your case. Chapter 7 and 13 trustees are appointed by the *United States Trustee*, an official of the Justice Department. In a Chapter 7 case the trustee represents the interests of the bankruptcy estate and the unsecured creditors. In most Chapter 7 cases the trustee does little except review your petition and schedules for inconsistencies and evidence of assets for creditors. In some Chapter 7 cases a trustee will object to exemptions or discharge.

The typical Chapter 7 debtor will not meet with the trustee unless the trustee raises an objection in the case. If you have been honest in your financial dealings, and you file Chapter 7, you probably have nothing to fear from your trustee.

Chapter 13 trustees have more responsibilities. Besides reviewing petitions and schedules, they review and evaluate the payment arrangements you make in your Chapter 13 plans. Their duties also include collecting and distributing plan payments.

■ Your Bankruptcy Judge

The court official who has all power over your bankruptcy case is your *bankruptcy judge*. Your bankruptcy judge may decide any matter connected with your case *including* whether you receive a discharge.

Your involvement with your bankruptcy judge may be limited. Although a Chapter 13 debtor may have to appear before the bankruptcy judge at the plan confirmation hearing, a typical Chapter 7 debtor will not see his judge unless an objection is raised in his case.

■ Property of Your Bankruptcy Estate

When you file a bankruptcy petition your *bankruptcy estate* is created. Generally speaking, your creditors will be paid from nonexempt property in your bankruptcy estate. Your bankruptcy estate consists of all the property belonging to you at the time you filed bankruptcy and includes property owned or held by another person if you have an interest in the property. (For example, if you have a mortgage on your brother's house, you have an interest in the house and that interest is part of your bankruptcy estate.) The items in the following list are examples of property of your bankruptcy estate if you owned or had an interest in them *before* you filed bankruptcy:

- Cash;
- Checking, savings, or other financial accounts;
- Certificates of deposit (CDs);
- Real property (including rental leases);
- Automobiles and other motor vehicles;
- Jewelry;
- Clothing;
- Other personal property (furniture, appliances, tools, cameras, stereos, etc.);
- Security deposits (to landlords, utilities, etc.);
- Insurance policies;
- Most non-ERISA (Employees Retirement Income Security Act) retirement plans (this depends on your state law and the law of your bankruptcy district);
- Pensions (depending on your state law and the law of your bankruptcy district);
- Tax refunds;
- Alimony, maintenance, or support payments;
- Securities and other financial instruments including promissory notes;
- Livestock;
- Intangibles (copyrights, patents);
- Anything owed to you.

EXAMPLES

Peter is injured by a doctor during surgery. Later, Peter files bankruptcy. Peter's claims against the doctor and hospital for malpractice are part of his bankruptcy estate. If he recovers money on the malpractice claim, that money is part of his bankruptcy estate.

Joan gave her friend Lisa money to buy a house and took a mortgage on the house. Later, Joan filed for bankruptcy. The mortgage is part of Joan's bankruptcy estate.

Certain property becomes property of your bankruptcy estate even if you acquire it after bankruptcy. For example, you might be lucky and get a windfall while you're in bankruptcy. Although the windfall comes to you after you've filed bankruptcy, it would be unfair to allow you to keep it from your creditors, so the Bankruptcy Code brings certain types of property you acquire *after* bankruptcy into your bankruptcy estate.

The following items are property of your bankruptcy estate if you obtained them or an interest in them within 180 days after you filed bankruptcy:

- Inherited property;
- Property from a marital settlement or divorce; or
- Life insurance or death benefits.

EXAMPLES

Bob files a Chapter 7 petition on March 1, 1993. On August 1, 1993, Bob's uncle Rufus dies and leaves Bob $100,000. This money is part of Bob's bankruptcy estate because he inherited it within 180 days of the date he filed his bankruptcy petition.

Mary sues her husband Peter for divorce on January 1, 1991. A little over one year later, on January 7, 1992, she files Chapter 7 bankruptcy. On June 1, 1992, the divorce becomes final. As part of the settlement, Mary gets a house Peter owned. The house becomes part of her bankruptcy estate because it is a marital/divorce settlement she received within 180 days after she filed bankruptcy.

**YOU MUST LIST ALL YOUR PROPERTY
IN YOUR SCHEDULES REGARDLESS OF
WHETHER OR NOT YOU FEEL THE PROPERTY
IS INCLUDABLE IN YOUR BANKRUPTCY ESTATE!**

■ Creditors' Claims

If people have a right to money or other payment from you *for any reason*, they hold *claims* against you. People who hold claims are *creditors*. Claims may be:

- **secured**. You have pledged property to a creditor to insure payment of a debt (for example, a mortgage on your home or car).
- **unsecured**. The creditor has no right to try to obtain any specific item of your property to satisfy your debt but has the right to make a claim against *you* for the debt.
- **contingent**. It is not certain that you owe the creditor anything, but you might owe him something (for example, you guaranteed or co-signed a loan).
- **liquidated**. The claim is for a specific amount.
- **unliquidated**. No specific value has been assigned to the claim.

EXAMPLES

Thomas owes ABC Bank $10,000 on his ABC Bank credit card. ABC Bank hired a lawyer to pursue Thomas when he failed to make the required monthly payments on the debt. The lawyer's fees totalled $800. Thomas files Chapter 7 bankruptcy. ABC Bank can file a claim against Thomas for $10,800. ABC Bank's claim is unsecured (because none of Thomas's property was pledged for the ABC Bank debt) and liquidated (because the claim is for a specific amount).

Billy, a six-year old boy, was struck and injured by a car Fred was driving. Fred was drunk at the time of the accident. Fred files Chapter 7 bankruptcy. Billy's claim against Fred is unsecured (because none of Fred's property has been pledged to Billy) and unliquidated (because Billy's claim for his injuries does not have a known value yet). If Fred had filed bankruptcy after Billy obtained a judgment against him, Billy's claim would be unsecured and liquidated.

Secured claims are satisfied from the property securing them. (The mortgaged property may be sold and the proceeds of the sale turned over to the creditor, or the property may be turned over to the creditor directly.)

Unsecured claims are paid from your nonexempt assets. Nonexempt assets are liquidated (sold), and the proceeds are used to pay the unsecured claims. In most consumer cases there is little or no nonexempt property. Nonexempt property usually has too little value to warrant an attempt to sell it, so debtors usually buy nonexempt property from the trustee. (The debtor will simply give the trustee the value of the property.)

All unsecured claims are not created equal; some are given *priority* status and are paid first. For example, claims for bankruptcy case administration, lawyers' fees and taxes have priority status. Nonpriority, general unsecured claims are treated equally.

■ Chapter 7 Procedure

In Chapter 7 cases, nonexempt property is left for creditors. Because there is usually little or no nonexempt property in consumer Chapter 7 cases, these cases are called *no-asset* cases. (Most unsecured creditors in consumer Chapter 7 cases receive less than ten cents on the dollar.)

A creditor holding an unsecured claim may get money from your bankruptcy estate only if your case is not a no-asset case and if the creditor files a *proof of claim* within the time specified by the bankruptcy court. A proof of claim describes the reason you owe the creditor money. Most creditors in Chapter 7 cases don't file proofs of claim because most Chapter 7 cases are no-asset cases. A proof of claim is evidence of a genuine debt and entitles a creditor to receive payment on the claim if the claim is *allowed.* A claim is allowed unless you (or another interested party) object to it. (Creditors whose claims are secured are not required to file proofs of claim, but many do so anyway.)

You get permanent relief from your debts when you receive a *discharge* from the bankruptcy court. You will receive a discharge of your dischargeable debts (debts which the bankruptcy court is authorized to discharge) unless:

(1) you have committed certain designated "bad acts" (*See Chapter Four*);

(2) an interested party successfully objects to your discharge;

(3) you do not complete all the procedures required in your case; or

(4) you received a discharge in another bankruptcy case that was started within six years prior to the date you filed your present bankruptcy case.

After you receive a discharge, you have no further personal liability on the discharged debts. This freedom from debt gives you your fresh start, the fundamental goal of Chapter 7 bankruptcy.

Your Chapter 7 case will probably follow this pattern:

(1) You file your Chapter 7 bankruptcy petition.

(2) You file your schedules within 15 days of filing your petition.

(3) A Chapter 7 trustee is appointed to your case.

(4) You appear before your creditors to be questioned (the "341" meeting). You will be notified of the date of this meeting on the bankruptcy notice sent to you by the court.

(5) Your creditors file proofs of claim (unless yours is a no-asset case).

(6) Your trustee files a "no-asset" report;

(7) You obtain a discharge (if no objection is made and the debts are dischargeable).

(8) Your nonexempt assets are distributed (if your case is not a no-asset case).

(9) Your case is closed and you are out of bankruptcy.

■ Chapter 13 Procedure

Your Chapter 13 case will probably proceed as follows:

(1) You file your Chapter 13 petition and plan.

(2) You file your schedules within 15 days of filing your petition.

(3) A Chapter 13 trustee is appointed.

(4) You appear before your creditors to be questioned and in some courts to discuss the contents of your proposed plan (the "341" meeting).

(5) Your creditors file proofs of claim.

(6) You obtain bankruptcy court approval of your plan ("confirmation"). Creditors can object to your proposed plan.

(7) You complete payments under the plan (over a three-year period unless the court agrees to more time).

(8) You obtain a discharge of your dischargeable debts.

The plan process is the heart of Chapter 13. Chapter 13 is intended to help you retain key assets (such as your home or small business) by paying off the debts you are behind on over time—usually three years. To obtain confirmation of your Chapter 13 plan, you must meet six conditions:

(1) Your plan must fully comply with the Bankruptcy Code.

(2) You must pay the required administrative fees.

(3) Your plan must be proposed in good faith and must not involve anything illegal.

(4) Your plan must give your unsecured creditors as much as they would get if you had filed under Chapter 7. (Remember: Most Chapter 7 cases are no-asset cases, and unsecured creditors usually get nothing.)

(5) Your secured creditors accept the plan *or* they retain their liens on your property and receive the value of their claims as estimated by the bankruptcy court *or* they receive the property securing their claims (you turn over the property to them).

(6) You convince the bankruptcy court that you can make all payments under the plan.

It will probably be easy for you to meet conditions (1) through (4). Condition (5) may cause you more difficulty because creditors may put up a fight. You'll notice that if secured creditors do not accept the plan, there are still two ways that you can deal with them. In the worst case, you can surrender the property to them. Or, what is better, you can fight them and possibly reduce the value of their claims. (*See Chapter Seven.*)

Condition (6) requires you to convince the bankruptcy judge and the Chapter 13 trustee that your plan is "feasible." To do this you must show that during the life of the plan you will have sufficient income (after paying taxes, food bills, mortgage payments, etc.) to make the required plan payments.

EXAMPLE
John is a Chapter 13 debtor. He is six months behind in his mortgage payments of $1,000 per month. He fell behind in his mortgage payments when he lost his job. He has recently found a job paying $150 a week more than his previous job. John must show the bankruptcy judge that he can pay the $6,000 off over time with his disposable income. Assuming the judge believes John when he says his new job is secure, the judge will probably confirm John's plan. In deciding whether John's plan is feasible, the judge will probably defer to the opinion of John's Chapter 13 trustee.

Because few people can say what the state of their lives will be three or five years ahead, Chapter 13 plans often must be "modified" — adjusted to accommodate changes in a debtor's financial life during the plan period. Sometimes plan payments will be reduced, or the life of the plan may be extended to five years if the debtor can show the court good reasons for doing so. Chapter 13 allows your bankruptcy judge the flexibility to modify your plan when necessary, as long as it remains reasonable and doesn't unfairly harm your creditors.

Sometimes an *un*secured creditor (or the Chapter 13 trustee) will object to a plan. An unsecured creditor may object to a plan because it gives nothing for the claim. (Remember: A Chapter 13 plan need only provide the creditor what would be provided in Chapter 7, which is usually nothing.) If a creditor raises an objection to your plan, the court will not approve the plan unless either the value the objecting creditor receives on the claim is at least as much as the value of the claim or *all* your disposable income for the plan period will be applied to plan payments.

Generally, all unsecured creditors must be treated equally under your plan. If they all get zero percent of their claims, then the plan cannot be for more than three years. If you are willing to pay 70% to 100% of the unsecured claims, then your plan period can be extended to up to five years. Generally, you will want to devise a plan that will allow you to keep your home and your car.

If creditors object to your plan, you can probably silence them by proving to the bankruptcy judge that all your disposable income during the plan period will go to making plan payments. Once you've done this, the bankruptcy judge will probably confirm your plan provided you satisfy the other confirmation requirements, which often includes making monthly payments for the time between when you file and when your plan is confirmed — about 45 to 60 days.

CHAPTER FOUR

Discharge

A *discharge* releases you from personal liability for your discharged debts and prevents your creditors from ever taking any action against you or your property to collect those debts. The discharge also prohibits your creditors from:

- making any communication regarding collection of the debt with you, your relatives, employees, or friends, including phone calls, letters, or personal contact; and

- acting against your property to collect a debt.

Both Chapter 7 and Chapter 13 allow debtors to discharge their debts. A discharge releases you from all your "dischargeable" debts. A debt is *dischargeable* if the bankruptcy court has the power to release you from your obligation to pay it. Certain debts are not dischargeable in either Chapter 7 or 13 bankruptcy. Those debts are described in Chapter Five. Chapter Four discusses whether a debtor is eligible for a discharge.

Discharge in Chapter 7

You will receive a discharge in Chapter 7 *unless* you do one or more of these things (sometimes called "bad acts"):

- You deliberately transfer, hide, or mutilate your property *in the year before* you file bankruptcy or do any of these acts to your estate property after you file bankruptcy in an attempt to defraud or hinder your creditors or your trustee.

- You conceal, destroy, falsify, mutilate, or fail to keep or preserve information (including books, records, and papers) concerning your financial affairs, unless your actions are justified under the circumstances.

- You are guilty of a bankruptcy crime (you lie or give false information in the bankruptcy case; you are guilty of extortion or bribery in the bankruptcy case; or you withhold documents concerning your financial affairs from your trustee or bankruptcy judge). All the documents you submit will be under oath and under penalty of perjury.

• You fail to explain the absence or loss of estate assets.

• You refuse, during the case, to obey a bankruptcy court order; you refuse to testify on the grounds of your Fifth Amendment privilege against self-incrimination after the bankruptcy court has granted you immunity from prosecution; or you refuse to testify on any grounds except your Fifth Amendment privilege against self-incrimination.

EXAMPLE
Robert is a Chapter 7 debtor. One of his creditors, Reliable Bank, objects to Robert's discharge. Reliable claims Robert secretly transferred assets to his wife, Helen, six months before he filed bankruptcy. At the court hearing on the objection, Robert refuses to answer questions about the transfers. Robert may be denied a discharge because of his refusal to testify.

• You committed any of the above acts within one year before you filed your bankruptcy petition, or during your case.

• You received a discharge in a Chapter 7 (or Chapter 11) case started within the past six years.

• You received a discharge in a Chapter 13 (or Chapter 12) case started within the past six years (the "six year bar") *unless* the unsecured creditors in the earlier case received 100% percent of their claims against you, or the unsecured creditors in the previous case received at least 70% of their claims and your plan was your best effort and you proposed it in good faith.

• You waive your discharge after you file bankruptcy.

• You reaffirm a debt. (*See "Reaffirmation: New Promises to Pay Your Old Debts" later in this chapter.*)

Because the purpose of Chapter 7 is to give you a "fresh start" without burdensome debts, all of the procedures of a Chapter 7 case are intended to culminate in a discharge of the debts that drove you into bankruptcy. For this reason, being denied a discharge is a very serious matter for you as a Chapter 7 debtor.

Denial of a discharge means that although you've filed bankruptcy, your creditors can continue to hound you for their money. It also means that although you have damaged your credit rating for ten years by filing bankruptcy, you will not receive all of its benefits.

Discharge In Chapter 13

Discharge has a different role in Chapter 13 cases. In Chapter 13, saving a debtor's valuable assets from creditors is as important as granting the discharge. To encourage people to file under Chapter 13 rather than Chapter 7 (because creditors usually get more money out of debtors in Chapter 13 cases), the Bankruptcy Code permits debtors to discharge some debts in Chapter 13 that are nondischargeable in Chapter 7.

Your Chapter 13 discharge is conditioned upon two things: you make all payments required under your Chapter 13 plan, *and* you pay all administrative claims, such as taxes, in full. The standards for a Chapter 7 discharge are irrelevant in Chapter 13 cases. This means that the deeds that would prevent you from receiving a discharge in Chapter 7 won't keep you from obtaining a Chapter 13 discharge. However, you won't obtain a Chapter 13 discharge if you file your case or plan in bad faith.

Reaffirmation: New Promises to Pay Your Old Debts

Occasionally a debtor will want to pay dischargeable debts. Why? Because the debtor may want to obtain credit or services from the creditor after bankruptcy. (For example, if a debtor owes a doctor money for services and the debt is discharged, the debtor may fear that the doctor will refuse to provide medical care in the future.) Also, sometimes debtors feel a moral obligation to pay as much as they can to creditors.

When a debtor makes a promise to pay a dischargeable debt the debtor *reaffirms* the debt. Because discharge is a fundamental part of the Bankruptcy Code, reaffirmation was not popular with Congress when considered for inclusion as an option in the Bankruptcy Code. Reaffirmation is equally unpopular with bankruptcy courts.

Because reaffirmation is such a serious step, the Bankruptcy Code imposes several requirements for debtors who wish to reaffirm debts:

- The reaffirmation agreement must be made before you receive your discharge;

- The reaffirmation agreement must contain a clear and conspicuous statement telling you that you can change your mind any time before discharge or within 60 days after the reaffirmation agreement is filed with the bankruptcy court, whichever is later;

- The agreement must be filed with the bankruptcy court and, if an attorney represented you during the negotiation of the agreement, the agreement must be accompanied by a declaration from your attorney stating that you entered the agreement voluntarily, you were fully informed about it, and the agreement does not impose an undue hardship on you. If you were not represented by an attorney during negotiation of the reaffirmation agreement, the bankruptcy court must find that the agreement does not impose an undue hardship on you and that it is in your best interests. (However, if the debt is a consumer debt secured by real property, the court does not need to make these findings.)

- You must not have cancelled the reaffirmation agreement;

- You must appear before the bankruptcy court for a hearing on the reaffirmation agreement.

Before the Bankruptcy Code was enacted, some creditors nagged or bullied debtors into reaffirming debts, often with disastrous results. Because of these abuses, Congress made reaffirmation something of an inconvenience for debtors to discourage them from giving in to creditors' demands. Congress also gave debtors the power to renege on reaffirmation agreements (within 60 days after the agreement is filed) to protect them in cases where honoring reaffirmation agreements becomes an unforeseen hardship.

Although creditors delight in reaffirmations, you should not reaffirm a debt just to make a creditor happy. *In most cases there is no need to reaffirm.* If you want to pay a creditor you can probably do so without making an enforceable and potentially burdensome promise.

CHAPTER FIVE

Nondischargeable Debts

A discharge only eliminates "dischargeable" debts. If a particular debt is *nondischargeable,* it survives bankruptcy and the creditor who is owed the debt may try to collect it from you or your property after you are out of bankruptcy. A debt that may be nondischargeable in Chapter 7 may be dischargeable in Chapter 13.

Unless stated otherwise, the following debts are not dischargeable under either Chapter 7 or 13:

Certain Taxes

The Bankruptcy Code provides that certain taxes are not dischargeable in bankruptcy. Here are the types of nondischargeable tax debts that present problems for most consumer debtors.

■ Any Tax

Any type of tax is nondischargeable if you were required to file a return and:

- you did not file the required return;
- you filed a fraudulent return;
- you filed a late return within two years before you filed bankruptcy; or
- you willfully attempted to evade or defeat the tax.

■ Income Taxes

Your income taxes are nondischargeable if:

- they became due within the three years before you filed bankruptcy;
- they were assessed against you within the 240 days before

you filed bankruptcy if they were a result of returns you filed within three years of the date of your last tax return; and
- they had not been assessed when you filed bankruptcy but were afterwards.

■ Withholding, Sales, or Other Tax You Were Required to Collect

If you were required to collect any tax and you failed to do so or to pay the collected tax to the governmental authority, any debts for the nonpayment are nondischargeable.

■ Property Taxes

If property taxes were assessed against you before you filed bankruptcy and were payable (without any penalties) before you filed, the debts for those taxes are nondischargeable.

> PENALTIES IMPOSED AGAINST YOU
> FOR NONDISCHARGEABLE TAXES ARE
> ALSO NONDISCHARGEABLE!

Money, Credit, Property or Services You Obtained Fraudulently

If you have debts for money, property, services, or any extension, renewal or refinancing of credit, they are *nondischargeable* in Chapter 7 to the extent you obtained them by:
- using fraud, false pretenses, or false representation to anyone *except about your financial condition (or the financial condition of a relative or a corporation for which you are a director, officer or person in control)*; or

- writing an intentionally false statement about your financial condition or the financial condition of a relative or a corporation for which you are a director, officer, or person in control, which caused a creditor to extend money, property, services, or credit.

EXAMPLE

Holly wanted an American Credit Card, but she was ineligible because The American Credit Card Company required a minimum annual income of $25,000 and Holly made only $18,000 per year. Holly lied on her American Credit Card application and said she made $50,000 per year. The American Credit Card Company issued an American Credit Card to Holly based on her lie about her salary.

Holly files Chapter 7 bankruptcy. She owes The American Credit Card Company $10,000 on her American Credit Card. Holly's debt to The American Credit Card Company is not dischargeable because she intentionally gave the company false information about her financial condition.

IF A CREDITOR DOES NOT SUCCESSFULLY
OBJECT TO A DISCHARGE ON THESE GROUNDS,
THE DEBT WILL BE DISCHARGED.

Luxury Goods or Services You Purchased or Cash Advances You Obtained Shortly Before Bankruptcy: "Spending Spree" Debts

If you incurred debts of $500 or more to one creditor for "luxury goods or services" (goods or services that are not basic necessities) within 40 days before you filed bankruptcy, or you obtained cash advances totalling $1,000 or more within 20 days before you filed, those debts are *presumed* to be nondischargeable in Chapter 7.

The logic behind this presumption is simple: If you buy luxury goods or borrow money on a credit card and file bankruptcy shortly thereafter, it can be assumed that you knew you would file bankruptcy when you incurred those debts. If your creditors had known you intended to file bankruptcy, they would not have given you the money or luxuries. This suggests that you deceived your creditors when you obtained the money or goods. You can attack this presumption by convincing the bankruptcy judge that you intended to pay for the luxuries or money when you obtained them.

EXAMPLES

On January 1, Alice buys $600 worth of jewelry at Saks Fifth Avenue on her Saks Fifth Avenue charge card. On February 1, Alice files her bankruptcy petition. The debt to Saks Fifth Avenue was for jewelry, a luxury item, and was incurred less than 40 days before Alice filed her Chapter 7 bankruptcy petition. The debt to Saks Fifth Avenue is presumed to be nondischargeable.

On January 1, Alice obtains a cash advance of $1,500 from her ABC Bank Visa card. On January 19th she files her Chapter 7 bankruptcy petition. The cash advance was incurred less than 20 days before Alice filed her bankruptcy petition. It is presumed that the $1,500 debt is nondischargeable.

In either of these examples, if the creditor objects to her discharge, Alice will have to convince her bankruptcy judge that she intended to pay the debts when she incurred them. Otherwise, the debts will not be discharged.

**IF A CREDITOR DOES NOT SUCCESSFULLY
OBJECT TO A DISCHARGE ON THESE GROUNDS,
THE DEBT WILL BE DISCHARGED.**

Debts Not Listed In Your Schedules

You are obligated to list *every one* of your creditors in your schedules. If you do not, you will not receive a discharge in Chapter 7 for any omitted creditor *who does not receive proper notice of your bankruptcy case.*

Fraud You Commited in a Fiduciary Capacity, Embezzlement, and Larceny

If you are responsible for other people's money or property and you defraud them, Chapter 7 does not allow you to discharge the debts you owe them. Similarly, if you embezzled money or property, you cannot discharge debts resulting from the embezzlement. Also, if you have debts resulting from a larceny you committed, you cannot discharge them in Chapter 7.

**IF A CREDITOR DOES NOT SUCCESSFULLY
OBJECT TO A DISCHARGE ON THESE GROUNDS,
THE DEBT WILL BE DISCHARGED.**

Alimony, Spousal Support, Maintenance, and Child Support

Debts you owe to a spouse, ex-spouse, or children as alimony, maintenance, or support are nondischargeable.

IF A CREDITOR DOES NOT SUCCESSFULLY OBJECT TO A DISCHARGE ON THESE GROUNDS, THE DEBT WILL BE DISCHARGED.

Debts for Willful or Malicious Injury to Person or Property

Debts you owe for willful or malicious injury to person or property are nondischargeable in Chapter 7.

Fines or Penalties Owed to a Governmental Unit, Including Restitution

If you owe money to a governmental unit (federal, state, or local) for a fine, penalty, or forfeiture, including restitution, that is not a tax or tax penalty, you cannot discharge the debt in Chapter 7.

EXAMPLE
Michele is a former welfare recipient. She committed welfare fraud by collecting welfare under a fictitious name. Her fraud was discovered, and she was ordered to make restitution. Michele files Chapter 7. She cannot discharge the restitution debt.

Student Loans

If you received or signed for guaranteed student loans, received an overpayment of educational benefits granted by a governmental unit, or received scholarships or stipends which require repayment, these debts are nondischargeable in either Chapter 7 or Chapter 13 bankruptcy *unless* the obligation to pay them became due at least seven years before you filed bankruptcy or you and your dependents will suffer undue hardship unless the debt is discharged.

> **EXAMPLE**
> *In September 1984, John obtained a $5,000 federally guaranteed student loan to take a one year auto repair training course. After completing the program in June 1985, John searched in vain for a job. In January, 1986 his student loan came due. Because he couldn't find work, he was unable to make the required payments on his student loan. John defaulted on the student loan and never received any deferrals from the bank which issued it. In March 1993, John filed Chapter 7 bankruptcy. His student loan is dischargeable because he filed bankruptcy more than seven years after his loan became due.*

Debts for Vehicular Accidents You Caused While You Were Driving Under the Influence

If you kill or injure someone while driving under the influence of drugs or alcohol, you cannot discharge the debt you owe the victim or victim's representative in either Chapter 7 or 13.

Debts You Could Have Listed in a Previous Bankruptcy Case

If you were a debtor in a previous bankruptcy case where you waived your discharge or were denied a discharge, any debts you list in your current case that were or could have been listed in the previous case are nondischargeable in Chapter 7.

Debts You Owe to the FDIC, FSLIC or the RTC

Debts you owe to the Federal Deposit Insurance Corporation (FDIC), Federal Savings and Loan Insurance Corporation (FSLIC), or Resolution Trust Corporation (RTC) for your malicious or reckless failure to maintain proper funding in a bank or thrift or for fraud or breach of fiduciary duty to any FDIC or FSLIC insured bank or thrift or an insured credit union are not dischargeable in Chapter 7.

Criminal Restitution

If you owe a restitution debt that was included in a criminal sentence imposed upon you, it is not dischargeable in Chapter 7 or 13.

CHAPTER SIX

Transfers of Your Property Before and After Bankruptcy

In the world of bankruptcy, a *transfer* is any means of sepa-rating you from your property. If you pay a debt, sell prop-erty, give a gift, or give a creditor a mortgage, you have trans-ferred your property to another. A transfer of your property by payment of a debt, a sale, or giving a gift is a *voluntary* transfer because your property was not taken from you.

If someone took your property from you without your con-sent, the transfer was *involuntary*. Tax liens and judgment liens are examples of involuntary transfers.

Transfers Before Bankruptcy

■ Preferential Debt Payments

Debt payments you made before you filed bankruptcy will be closely examined by your bankruptcy trustee, and the creditors who received the payments may be required to return them to the trustee.

A creditor who received payment before you filed bank-ruptcy will probably have to return the money received if the payment (or payments) totalled $600 or more.

Does this mean that *any* creditor you ever paid $600 or more could be forced to return the payment? No. Only payments made to *insiders* (relatives or business associates) within one year before you filed bankruptcy or to anyone within 90 days before you filed bankruptcy.

Such payments are called *preferential* because these creditors received more than your other creditors will through your bank-ruptcy. These creditors improved their position (or you improved it for them) at the expense of your other creditors. In bankruptcy, creditors are supposed to stand in line and receive payment according to the rules in the Bankruptcy Code. Preferential payments are forbidden by the Bankruptcy Code because they interfere with its policy of equal distribution among creditors.

Debt payments to an insider within one year before you filed bankruptcy may have to be returned to your bankruptcy trustee. Why a year before bankruptcy if the recipient was a relative or business associate? First, because you are more likely to pay people you care about before you pay your other creditors, and, second, these people are likely to know if you are in financial trouble before your other creditors do.

EXAMPLE

The recession has hit Mike's plumbing business hard. He knows he may have to file bankruptcy. His brother John loaned him $50,000 in 1990 to keep his business afloat. On January 2, 1992, Mike lays off most of his employees and repays his brother the $50,000. Mike has other creditors he should pay, but he wants to pay his brother first. On December 29, 1992, Mike files Chapter 13 bankruptcy. His Chapter 13 trustee calls John and demands that he return the $50,000 payment.

Mike's payment to John was a preferential payment because Mike does not have enough money to pay his other creditors *and* the payment was more than $600.

■ Fraudulent Transfers

When people take or receive your property and you get nothing for it, or you get less than what the property is worth, they may have received what are called *fraudulent transfers.* Why are these transfers "fraudulent?" Because in the real world you don't get something for nothing or get something without giving something of equal value in return.

Many people facing bankruptcy "sell" their property to relatives for little or nothing just to place the property beyond the reach of their creditors. Such "sales" are not genuine, and they will not protect property from the bankruptcy trustee.

Transfers of your property (by sale, gift, or other means) within the year before bankruptcy may also be fraudulent. Generally speaking, your trustee will not be interested in recovering small transfers unless there were many of them and they add up to a significant amount of money or property.

Sometimes a debtor will anticipate bankruptcy years in advance and will transfer property into friendly hands to thwart creditors. Although the Bankruptcy Code allows your trustee to recover fraudulent transfers made within one year of your bankruptcy filing, it also allows your trustee to use any available state law to recover your fraudulently transferred property. Some states have fraudulent transfer laws that allow recovery of property transferred many years before bankruptcy is filed.

EXAMPLE

Karl lives in New York. Jerry sued him for personal injuries in 1990. Karl knew from the beginning that Jerry had a good case and would probably win. Afraid of losing his property, Karl transferred his house to his brother, Ralph, and his stock to his daughter, Daphne. In January 1993, Jerry won the suit. In February 1993, Karl filed bankruptcy. Karl's bankruptcy trustee can recover both the house and the stock for Karl's bankruptcy estate because the New York fraudulent transfer law allows a bankruptcy trustee to recover property transferred as far back as six years before the debtor filed bankruptcy.

A few more words about fraudulent transfers: If you transfer your property before you file bankruptcy with the intent to hinder, delay, or defraud your creditors, you may be denied a discharge. (*See Chapter Four.*)

Transfers After Bankruptcy

Property of your bankruptcy estate cannot be used or transferred at will. If property of your estate is transferred without permission from the bankruptcy court, your trustee can recover it. For example, if you wrote a check before you filed bankruptcy, but it was paid by your bank after you filed, the trustee may be able to recover the payment.

Chapter Seven

Evictions and Related Matters

Unlawful Detainer Debtors

In some parts of the country, bankruptcy cases frequently result from eviction proceedings against tenants for failure to pay rent. Sometimes tenants who have received notices of eviction will seek bankruptcy protection to use the automatic stay to remain in their homes.

As stated in Chapter Two, the automatic stay prohibits interference with your property rights. As a tenant, you have a legal right to occupy, or "possess," your dwelling. This right of possession is a property right. However, if your landlord brings an *unlawful detainer action* against you and obtains an eviction order, your lease is terminated. (An unlawful detainer action is a lawsuit brought by a landlord against a tenant to evict the tenant—usually for nonpayment of rent.)

Once your lease is terminated, it is questionable whether you have *any* property interest in the dwelling. If you remain on the premises, you are certainly in possession of the dwelling, but does your mere presence in the dwelling give you a "right of possession" that is protected by the automatic stay? This question is still debated by bankruptcy judges.

The answer is probably irrelevant, however, because when your landlord receives notice that you have filed bankruptcy, he will make a motion before the bankruptcy court to lift the automatic stay in order to proceed with the eviction. Almost without exception, these requests are granted.

■ Bankruptcy Mills

If an unlawful detainer action has been brought against you and you have been told to vacate your dwelling within a certain time or be evicted, your name will appear among the records of the court that issued the eviction order. These eviction orders are public records open to everyone. Afterwards, you may be contacted by people who have found your name and who will offer you a chance to remain in your home.

These people represent *bankruptcy mills* and will tell you that for a few hundred dollars you may remain in your apartment for a few more weeks or even months by filing bankruptcy. They will offer to handle the bankruptcy filing process for a fee. Desperation prompts many people to pay for the chance of a few more weeks of housing. The bankruptcy mills often do not explain the consequences of bankruptcy (such as damage to the tenant's credit rating for at least 10 years) and sometimes they do not even tell tenants that they will be filing bankruptcy. Most of these desperate tenants find their bankruptcy cases dismissed by the bankruptcy court within 15 days because of their failure to file schedules.

The requirement that schedules be filed within 15 days of the petition date is strictly enforced. Bankruptcy petitions by debtors who are unlawful detainers are commonly called *face sheet filings* because they do not contain the required schedules, or, if they do, usually the landlord is the only creditor listed. Because most unlawful detainer debtors are poor people who cannot get credit, they do not have many creditors. (Indeed, some do not have bank accounts.) Sometimes they will list other creditors such as a utility, telephone company, or hospital. It is very sad to see these people come into court to beg a bankruptcy judge for more time to remain in an apartment. The money they gave the bankruptcy mill would have been better spent obtaining new housing.

Bankruptcy judges rarely give these people a break. In most cases, a bankruptcy judge will deny a motion from a landlord to lift the automatic stay *only* if the landlord fails to give the debtor proper notice of the court hearing on the motion. If the landlord *does* fail to give proper notice, and the court denies relief from the automatic stay, the landlord will then obtain a new hearing date for the motion and will give the debtor proper notice of the new hearing date.

Sooner or later a bankruptcy debtor will be evicted for non-payment of rent unless he makes up the past due rent payments or gives his landlord adequate assurance that the rent will be paid in the near future. There are other ways to avoid eviction, however, and these strategies are discussed in Chapter Eleven.

Bankruptcy After Mortgage Foreclosure

Although bankruptcy will probably be of little use if you are a renter facing eviction, it may help if you're facing eviction after foreclosure on your home mortgage.

Some, not all, federal courts say a debtor in bankruptcy has no right to *cure* (pay off) defaults under a mortgage after fore-closure. (Even Chapter 13 may not help you to recover your home if your bankruptcy judge decides that the law won't allow you to cure defaults.) Although your rights after foreclosure are generally determined by your state's law, your bankruptcy judge will decide whether you have this right.

If you can't cure your mortgage defaults because of a fore-closure, you may still have a right to *redeem* your property by paying off the entire mortgage debt, but for most debtors this is impossible. (That's why it is so important for you to consult with a bankruptcy lawyer before foreclosure!)

There may be another way to recover your home. If it was sold at the foreclosure sale for less than you believe it is worth, your bankruptcy lawyer may try to attack the foreclosure sale as a fraudulent transfer. (*For details about fraudulent transfers, see Chapter Six.*)

CHAPTER EIGHT

Bankruptcy Crimes

You must be truthful about everything concerning your bankruptcy case, including completion of court documents and answering questions asked by the bankruptcy judge, the trustees, and your lawyer. You also have an ongoing duty to volunteer information to your lawyer or trustee about anything that materially affects your case.

Deception or "bad acts" before or during your bankruptcy case can cost you your discharge. Being denied a discharge is no joke. Not only can your creditors continue to hound you for debts, but you will have damaged your credit rating for nothing just by filing bankruptcy. Although being denied a discharge is a disaster, there are even worse consequences for dishonesty and fraud: you may be found guilty of a *bankruptcy crime*.

If you commit a bankruptcy crime, you will be in danger of much more than a denial of discharge: you will be in danger of criminal prosecution. If convicted of a bankruptcy crime, you can be sent to prison and fined. Owing money is terrible, but prison is much worse.

If you knowingly and fraudulently do any of the following, you will commit a bankruptcy crime:

- You deliberately conceal assets before or during your case;

- You lie in connection with your case;

- You make a false declaration, statement, certification, or verification in connection with your case;

- You file a fraudulent proof of claim;

- You give or take a bribe in connection with your case; or

- You conceal, withhold, destroy, mutilate, falsify, or make a false entry in any record concerning your property or financial affairs.

EXAMPLE

Fred knows that he must file bankruptcy soon. He knows that in bankruptcy he will lose the house he inherited from his father last year because his exemptions will not allow him to keep it. Fred's father died without a will, and although Fred inherits the property as next of kin, title to the property is not in his name yet. Fred deliberately omits the property from his bankruptcy schedules. Fred thinks his bankruptcy trustee won't be able to find the property because it is not in his name.

Fred has committed a bankruptcy crime. He has knowingly (he knew his actions were illegal) and willfully (he lied deliberately) hidden his property from his bankruptcy trustee and creditors. Fred can be imprisoned for up to five years and fined up to $5,000. In the process of committing the bankruptcy crime he may also have violated other federal or state laws. Although most dishonest debtors are smart enough to know they can't bribe a trustee—and don't try—many are not above hiding their assets or "selling" them to their relatives for little or nothing. It should be clear to you that bankruptcy relief and discharge are not rights, but privileges. These privileges can be lost through dishonesty and fraud. It is in your interest to avoid even the appearance of impropriety. If you are in doubt about the honesty of your actions, ask your bankruptcy lawyer for advice.

Don't try to get away with anything in bankruptcy. Your trustee knows every trick and scam, and you won't get away with dishonesty.

CHAPTER NINE

You and Your Bankruptcy Lawyer

Why You Should Hire a Bankruptcy Lawyer

Bankruptcy is a specialized area of law containing many traps even for experienced bankruptcy lawyers. For this reason, nonlawyers should not file bankruptcy on their own. Unfortunately, many people are advised to file bankruptcy without the assistance of a lawyer. Such advice usually comes from people who sell "how to file bankruptcy" kits and others who make money by promoting "self-help" bankruptcies. Although hiring a bankruptcy lawyer costs money, the benefits of competent bankruptcy counsel far outweigh the expense. An experienced bankruptcy lawyer will help you by:

- making sure your court papers are complete and filed on time;

- using the law to your advantage; and

- protecting you, to the extent possible, if your trustee and/or creditors try to prevent you from obtaining a discharge, exempting your assets, or keeping your property.

Furthermore, an experienced consumer bankruptcy attorney can advise you about how to "plan" your bankruptcy case. For example, she might show you how to convert nondischargeable debt into dischargeable debt. She might also advise you to delay filing bankruptcy if you are expecting a large debt that could be discharged along with your other debts.

Bankruptcy, like many things, can be manipulated to your advantage. You will have to live with the effects of bankruptcy for many years, so you should get as much out of it as you can. The easiest and surest way to do this is by using a qualified consumer bankruptcy lawyer.

How To Find A Bankruptcy Lawyer

Most lawyers specialize in a particular area of law. Some claim to specialize in several: telephone books are full of advertisements by lawyers who make such claims. It takes a long time to become an expert in an area of law, and I am skeptical of anyone who would say something like: "I advise clients in matrimonial, criminal, bankruptcy, and personal injury matters." Although it is possible for a lawyer to practice in many legal areas, some lawyers do it simply to make themselves more marketable to prospective clients. By so doing they further their interests, not yours.

Some lawyers offer free initial consultations. View these offers as sales "come ons" designed to benefit the seller (i.e., the lawyer), not you. Such meetings tend to be short because the lawyer isn't receiving anything for his time.

Because a lawyer won't get any money from you unless you file bankruptcy, you should be wary of lawyers who push you towards bankruptcy and don't discuss nonbankruptcy solutions to your financial problems. A lawyer is supposed to tell his clients what's best for them, not further his own financial interests. An ethical lawyer will tell you whether bankruptcy is the solution to your problems.

You should find a lawyer specializing in consumer bankruptcy law. A consumer bankruptcy specialist will be privy to the current state of federal and state laws affecting consumer bankruptcy cases and can offer you the best help. Some states certify lawyers as specialists. To receive certification as a consumer bankruptcy specialist, a lawyer must have practiced bankruptcy for at least five years and must have passed a rigorous certification examination. If your state *does* certify lawyers as consumer bankruptcy specialists (you can find out from your state's bar association), you should seek one of these attorneys.

It is not difficult to find a qualified consumer bankruptcy lawyer. Never choose a lawyer from a telephone book or a paid advertisement. Don't do it even if the lawyer (or law firm) advertises himself as a certified bankruptcy specialist. Would you choose your baby's pediatrician from a telephone book?

There are several ways to find a good bankruptcy lawyer. In my opinion, the best way is to contact your local nonprofit consumer credit counseling center and ask if they will handle your bankruptcy case. To find the nonprofit consumer credit counseling service (CCCS) near you, call 1-800-388-CCCS. (You should arrange a meeting with your local CCCS for debt counseling as soon as possible whether or not you think you should file bankruptcy. The fee for their debt counseling services is nominal—about $30— and with help from your CCCS you may be able to avoid bankruptcy!) The CCCS would probably handle your bankruptcy case for about $400, far less than most private lawyers charge.

Another way to find a bankruptcy lawyer (although it is probably a difficult one) is to get a referral from a Chapter 7 or 13 trustee. Chapter 7 and 13 trustees regularly see bankruptcy lawyers in court and they know who the good ones are.

The way to get in contact with the Chapter 7 and 13 trustees is through the United States Trustee's office. You may obtain the address and phone number of the United States Trustee's office for your federal district from your bankruptcy court's clerk's office. However, do not ask bankruptcy court personnel for the names of the trustees because it is unlikely they will give you that information. DO NOT ASK BANKRUPTCY COURT PERSONNEL TO RECOMMEND LAWYERS! They can't and won't.

Once you've contacted the United States Trustee's office, ask for the names and numbers of a few of the most approachable Chapter 7 or 13 trustees. If the United States Trustee's office asks why you need this information, say that you need a referral to a good consumer bankruptcy lawyer. Then call the Chapter 7 or 13 trustees and ask them to recommend lawyers who will suit your needs.

Bar associations are another good, though less reliable, source of lawyer referrals. They will usually recommend attorneys upon request. Ask for several names.

Bankruptcy Sharks

Before you hire a particular lawyer, you might consider contacting the state bar to learn if she has ever been disciplined for improper or questionable conduct. Do not assume that a lawyer (even one who has been recommended to you) is honest. Every profession has dishonest members, and there are a number of lawyers, eager to cash in on the present bankruptcy bonanza, who simply cannot be trusted.

You should also be on your guard against nonlawyers who either misrepresent themselves as lawyers, or who admit they are not lawyers, but offer to handle your case anyway. These nonlawyers run businesses they officially describe as *typing services* that prepare bankruptcy petitions. These typing services usually charge between $100 and $200 to prepare a bankruptcy petition. People who operate such typing services are engaging in the unauthorized practice of law and can be punished for it. Also, they can be ordered by a bankruptcy court to refund money they charged to prepare petitions.

For an example of how a typing service may be forced to refund money received for preparing bankruptcy petitions, read the bankruptcy court decision in Appendix B, *In re Bachmann*. The decision describes the activities of a typing service, Capital Business Services, that advertised in several Florida newspapers. The man who owned and operated Capital, Paul C. Meyer, was not a lawyer. Capital charged between $85 and $160 to prepare bankruptcy petitions. Capital prepared a Chapter 13 petition and a Chapter 13 plan for the debtors, a Florida couple, and charged them $110.

The debtors ran into trouble in their Chapter 13 case because Capital had improperly prepared their Chapter 13 plan. They admitted to their bankruptcy judge that they knew nothing about bankruptcy and told him that Capital had prepared their petition and plan. The judge ordered Paul Meyer to appear before him to explain why, as a nonlawyer, he was preparing bankruptcy petitions and plans. The bankruptcy judge determined that Meyer was practicing law without a license and ordered him to stop. The bankruptcy judge also ordered Meyer to refund $50 of the money the debtors had paid Capital.

It is clearly the law now that typing services cannot give any assistance other than typing petitions. They cannot, for instance, instruct people as to how petitions are to be completed. Furthermore, the amount they charge for their services may be limited.

You should also read the bankruptcy court decision in Appendix C, *In re Davis & Associates, P.C.* This decision describes one of the most extreme examples of victimization of debtors by lawyers and nonlawyers. The decision concerns a law firm that was forced into bankruptcy because the man who owned the firm (and who isn't a lawyer) left the firm and took the firm's clients' money with him.

The firm, Davis & Associates, P.C. of San Antonio, Texas, advertised itself on national news programs as an established firm of well-qualified bankruptcy lawyers. This was a lie because the only lawyer in the firm practicing bankruptcy law had no significant bankruptcy experience, and much of the work was done by paralegals. Ultimately, the bankruptcy judge presiding over the firm's case barred the firm from practicing law in the bankruptcy courts in the Western District of Texas. I have met other bankruptcy judges who have barred dishonest or incompetent lawyers and firms from practicing in their courts.

As I said before, do not hire a lawyer or law firm because of their advertising. Remember: Paid advertising is nothing more than self-promotion. Self-promoters make self-serving statements about their credentials and qualifications. View them with suspicion, and find yourself a lawyer from referrals.

Working With Your Bankruptcy Lawyer

Question your prospective lawyer carefully. Ask him how long he has practiced consumer bankruptcy and whether he thinks your case may present problems. If he knows his business, he'll ask you probing questions about your financial dealings to find out if you may have difficulty discharging some or all of your debts.

This interview is not the time to be coy or untruthful. The lawyer needs to know as much about your debts as possible. He should have a list of questions to ask you about your debts, and you should be suspicious if he does not. A good lawyer will tell you up front which debts can be discharged and why others cannot.

Some competent and honest lawyers delegate the majority of the work in consumer bankruptcy cases to paralegals or secretaries. They justify this outrageous practice as a necessity by claiming that they are "too busy" to handle "routine" details and their time is better spent on other matters. No client should stand for this. What the lawyer means is that his time is too valuable to give to an insignificant consumer debtor and it is more profitable for him to spend his time collecting large hourly fees from more wealthy clients.

The bankruptcy process may be "routine" for your lawyer, but it is a very serious matter for you. It is one thing to have a paralegal or secretary present at meetings to record information, but quite another to have a paralegal working as the lawyer in one of the most important legal matters in your life. Some paralegals have told me that the bankruptcy lawyers for whom they work don't even read the petitions they sign! If this happens to you, stand your ground and tell your lawyer you have paid for his services and you want his attention.

The way a prospective attorney treats you is a good indicator of how he'll treat you once you've hired him. If he keeps you waiting in the reception area when you visit his office; puts you on hold for long periods of time when you telephone him; accepts calls or other interruptions during your meeting with him; does not return your calls promptly; rushes through the first meeting with you; or delegates all tasks concerning your case to his secretary or paralegal, it is safe to assume that he will continue to do these things after you've hired and paid him.

Once you've hired your lawyer, don't assume you can leave everything to him. Lawyers, even the best ones, are human and commit errors. Before any deadline or court hearing date, call your lawyer to make sure he knows about the deadline or hearing date and will handle the matter. Even experienced lawyers occasionally forget hearing dates. Don't worry about what your lawyer thinks of your reminders. He works for you and you are protecting your interests by keeping him on his toes.

In addition to reminding your lawyer about his duties, you should keep him informed about anything that affects your bankruptcy case. For example, if your car is part of your bankruptcy estate and it is stolen, inform your bankruptcy lawyer and your trustee immediately.

Regular, truthful communication with your lawyer will make it easier for him to help you and will help you get the most out of bankruptcy.

Lawyers' Fees

Most lawyers charge a flat fee for handling Chapter 7 cases, and many charge at least $700. Lawyers usually charge more for Chapter 13 cases. In addition to your lawyer's fee, you must pay a filing fee when you file your bankruptcy petition. At the time of this writing, the filing fee for a Chapter 7 or 13 case is $150 ($120 for the petition and $30 for the administration fee).

For an experienced consumer bankruptcy lawyer, a simple Chapter 7 case does not require much time. (Chapter 13 cases tend to require more time because a plan must be formulated and filed.) Whether your lawyer's fee is reasonable or excessive depends upon the amount and quality of time she spends on your case. For example, if your lawyer charges $1,000, including the filing fee, her take would be $850. If she has to put in six hours of work on the case, she will receive about $141.67 for each hour's work exclusive of overhead costs ($850 ÷ 6 = $141.67).

On the other hand, if difficulties arise your lawyer may be required to expend considerably more time on your case, and the case may not be profitable for her. If, for example, a creditor objects to your discharge, the objection creates an adversary proceeding—a lawsuit in bankruptcy court—that can be lengthy and troublesome. This would require your lawyer to draft papers to address the creditor's objection and could mean she would end up spending much more time on your case than originally estimated.

Most lawyers try to protect themselves from losing money by stating up front that certain types of work are not included in the basic fee. You should be sure to find out exactly how much work your lawyer thinks will be necessary and how much it will cost. Fees can vary widely among lawyers, so it pays to shop around.

If, after your case begins, you and your lawyer see that the case will be more complicated than anticipated, your lawyer may want to charge you more money than you initially agreed on, and chances are you may not have the additional money she demands. If you cannot pay your lawyer, she can't just drop your case. Most nonlawyers don't know this, but a lawyer has an obligation to handle a case so that her client's rights won't be harmed—even if her client can't pay the legal fee. Your lawyer is obligated to continue making court appearances and filing papers necessary to protect your rights until you get a new lawyer or the bankruptcy court releases her from your case.

■ Excessive Lawyers' Fees

Depending on the amount and quality of work your lawyer does in your case, you may think he has overcharged you. *You can ask your bankruptcy judge to determine whether the fee you paid your lawyer is excessive.*

Few debtors know that they have the right to ask their bankruptcy judge to compel their attorneys to refund fees: lawyers certainly don't tell them! This may be a powerful weapon for you. Bankruptcy judges have told me they would order refunds in many cases they oversee, but debtors don't request them.

If your bankruptcy judge decides your lawyer's fee is excessive, the judge can cancel the fee arrangement; deny your attorney any compensation; or order your attorney to return the excessive portion of the fees paid to your bankruptcy estate (if the money was estate property) or to whoever paid the fee.

The easiest way to make the request for a refund is to contact your Chapter 7 or 13 trustee and ask him to ask your bankruptcy judge to determine if the fees you paid to your lawyer are excessive. You can also ask this of the United States Trustee. It's best to make your request to your trustee or the United States Trustee in writing and to send a copy of the letter directly to your bankruptcy judge. (**Caution:** Some bankruptcy judges do not like to receive letters or communications regarding cases before them. To avoid angering your bankruptcy judge, you should probably contact his chambers and ask his law clerk if it would be all right to send a copy of your letter to the judge.) Be sure to put your case name (*In re Your Name*) and case number on any correspondence regarding your case!

Make a *cc* notation (*cc: Judge's Name*) on your letter so that when your trustee or the United States Trustee reads the letter he will know that the judge also received a copy. This should be effective in getting the trustee to move quickly.

CHAPTER TEN

Filing Chapter 7 Bankruptcy on Your Own

I f you choose to disregard my advice and file bankruptcy without a lawyer, please reconsider your decision and change your mind. If, after further consideration, you *still* decide to file bankruptcy on your own, please read this chapter carefully.

If you intend to file Chapter 13 bankruptcy, this chapter is not for you. Rarely do debtors successfully complete Chapter 13 cases on their own, but if you elect to try it, obtain *Consumer Bankruptcy Law and Practice* (4th ed., 1992). This book is designed for lawyers and paralegals and can be obtained from the National Consumer Law Center, 11 Beacon Street, Boston, Massachusetts 02108, 617-523-8010. It sells for about $80 and contains most of the information you will need to file Chapter 13 on your own. (It does not, however, contain information about state exemptions law.)

To file your Chapter 7 case without a lawyer you need the proper forms and information about your exemptions options. You will also need to be very organized—there are many forms to complete and much information to keep track of.

Although I disapprove of self-help legal kits, if you must use one I recommend *How to File Bankruptcy* (Nolo Press, 950 Parker St., Berkeley, CA 94710-9867, 1-800-992-6656). This kit contains virtually everything you need to file your Chapter 7 petition, including the forms and your state's exemptions laws.

Bankruptcy Forms

■ The Bankruptcy Petition

The most important piece of paper in any bankruptcy case is the one that starts the case: the ***bankruptcy petition***. There is one

Official Form for all bankruptcy petitions regardless of the chapter under which the petition is filed. A copy of this form is included in Appendix A. As you will see, for a consumer debtor, a petition is only two pages long and is simple and straightforward.

■ Schedules and Statements

In addition to your petition, you must file several other papers:

(1) a list of the names and addresses of all your creditors (you don't have to file this list if you file your schedules with your petition);

(2) a schedule of your assets and liabilities;

(3) a schedule of your current income and expenditures;

(4) a schedule of executory contracts and unexpired leases to which you are a party;

(5) a statement of financial affairs;

(6) a statement of intention (only if you have secured debts);

(7) a master mailing list ("matrix").

A copy of the Official Form for each of these documents is included in Appendix A. The schedules, numbered (2) - (5) above, can be filed within 15 days of the petition date.

Statement of Intention

If you have secured debts, you must file a *statement of intention* that lists property securing your consumer debts. It describes your interest in each piece of property and your intentions concerning it. In this statement you declare, for each piece of secured property, whether you will *exempt* your interest in it, *redeem* it by paying the creditor its value (not the amount of the debt), or *surrender* it to the creditor.

The statement of intention must be filed within 30 days of the petition date or on or before the date of the 341 meeting (the meeting with your creditors), whichever comes first. A copy of the statement of intention must be served on the Chapter 7 trustee and the creditors you name in the statement before or after you file the statement.

You will notice I said "served on," not "sent to." *Serving* the statement of intention means sending a copy of the statement of intention in a *responsible manner* (such as by certified mail, return receipt requested or by messenger) to each creditor or creditor's representative listed on it. (Sending a statement of intention by regular mail is acceptable, but will not provide you with a signed receipt.)

When you file the statement of intention with the bankruptcy court, you should attach a *proof of service* to it. A proof of service is a statement that tells what was served, whom it was sent to, and the means by which it was sent. YOU CAN NEITHER EXECUTE THE PROOF OF SERVICE NOR SERVE THE STATEMENT OF INTENTION YOURSELF. Service must be made by someone at least 18 years of age who has no interest in your case or in the property listed in the statement of intention.

EXAMPLE

PROOF OF SERVICE

I, Peter Smith, caused the attached statement of intention to be served by certified mail on May 1, 1993, on the following persons: Marcy Davis, Esq., Simon, Crane & Gill, Attorneys for John Debtor, 666 Shark's Row, Milltown, NY 01234; ABC Bank, 1234 Main Street, Milltown, NY 01234, ATT: Peter Simplemind; Bill's CarLand, 301 South Tower Avenue, Milltown, NY 01232, ATT: Monica LeTour; St. Jude's Hospital, 321 Thompson Street, Milltown, NY 01236, ATT: Billing Department; EZ Furniture Co., 20 Main Street, Milltown, NY 01236; American Credit Card Co., 1000 Executive Drive, Colfax, ND 87000; Dr. James Smith, 370 LaVerne Avenue, Milltown, NY 01235; Le Chic Dress Shop, 51 Main Street, Milltown, NY 01236; Wilson's Pharmacy, 49 Main Street, Milltown, NY 01235; Kiddie Time Day Care, 100 Jones Drive, Milltown, NY 01236. I further certify that I am over 18 years of age and not a party to this bankruptcy case.   Signed: Peter Smith

---

Master Mailing List or "Matrix"

Some bankruptcy courts require debtors to provide a master mailing list of creditors, or *matrix.* (*See sample on next page.*)

A matrix is used to make labels for the notice letters that the bankruptcy court sends to creditors informing them that you've filed bankruptcy. This device saves bankruptcy court clerks' offices lots of work and is required by most bankruptcy courts.

```
John Debtor              Marcy Davis, Esq.        ABC Bank
101 South Main Street    Simon, Crane & Gill      1234 Main Street
Milltown, NY 01235       Attorneys for J. Debtor  Milltown, NY 01234
                         666 Shark's Row          ATT: Peter Simplemind
                         Milltown, NY 01234


Bill's CarLand           St. Jude's Hospital      EZ Furniture Co.
301 South Tower Avenue   321 Thompson Street      20 Main Street
Milltown, NY 01232       Milltown, NY 01236       Milltown, NY 01236
ATT: Monica LeTour       ATT: Billing Department


American Credit Card Co. Dr. James Smith          Le Chic Dress Shop
1000 Executive Drive     370 LaVerne Avenue       51 Main Street
Colfax, ND 87000         Milltown, NY 01235       Milltown, NY 01236
```

Sample Matrix

**YOU MAY BE REQUIRED TO FILE FORMS OR
DOCUMENTS NOT DISCUSSED HERE. WHEN YOU VISIT
THE BANKRUPTCY COURT BEFORE YOUR PETITION DATE,
ASK ABOUT REQUIRED FORMS AND STATEMENTS!**

Your Exemptions Options

Review Chapter Two's discussion of exemptions options.
Then follow the instructions in *How to File Bankruptcy* to complete your bankruptcy schedules.

As you work on the schedules, be sure to correctly name
each statute (and its sections and subsections) giving you the
right to exempt specific property.

EXAMPLE

*Joy is a debtor who lives in New York. New York debtors are limited
to New York's state exemptions. Joy's car is worth $3,000 and she
owns it outright. New York allows a debtor to exempt up to $2,400 in
a car. Joy can exempt $2,400 of her equity—the maximum allowed by
the statute. The statute that authorizes this is N.Y. Debtor & Creditor
Law 282 § (iii)(1). On Schedule 'C' of her bankruptcy schedules, Joy
will state: (1) the make and year of the car; (2) the law providing the
exemption— N.Y. Debt. & Cred. Law 282 § (iii)(1); (3) the value of
the exemption; and (4) the current market value of the car.*

Staying Organized

You will need to carefully plan and time your bankruptcy filing in order to take maximum advantage of the benefits of bankruptcy. To make your plans, you must know your deadline for filing bankruptcy and must conduct all necessary prebankruptcy planning in advance of the deadline.

Review the section in Chapter Two about prebankruptcy planning. You will have to use your best judgment about what steps you can take to obtain the most from your exemptions. (Remember: You must obtain information about your state law exemptions, if any, before you can plan your bankruptcy case.) As you conduct your prebankruptcy planning, I caution you again: *Any acts you take to hinder, delay, or defraud your creditors may cause you to be denied a discharge (see Chapter Four); and transfers of your property before bankruptcy with intent to hinder, delay or defraud your creditors can have the same result.*

■ Before You File

(1) Gather all your financial records. You should have at hand all information about your debts and property.

(2) Obtain *How to File Bankruptcy*. It contains a bankruptcy petition and other forms. It also contains excellent, detailed instructions and your state's exemptions law, if any. Bankruptcy forms are also available at any good commercial stationery store for $10 to $15; however, they usually aren't accompanied by instructions or state exemptions law information. Gather the information you need to complete the forms and complete them carefully.

(3) Visit the bankruptcy court before you file. Ask the bankruptcy court clerk's office personnel to tell you what you need to file your Chapter 7 petition. They will tell you the acceptable methods of paying the filing fee (certified check, money order, cash, etc.); what papers must be filed with

the petition; how many copies of the petition and other papers should be submitted; and the appropriate form of the petition and other necessary papers.

Visiting the bankruptcy court before you file is an important part of your prebankruptcy planning. In addition to the useful information you'll obtain from the bankruptcy court clerk's office, you'll learn the exact location of the clerk's office. This is very important, because you may have to rush at the last minute to file your petition.

(4) Be courteous to the bankruptcy court clerk staff. They work hard, and your courtesy and patience will be greatly appreciated.

DO NOT ASK THE BANKRUPTCY COURT CLERK PERSONNEL FOR LEGAL ADVICE!

■ At the Time You File

(1) Arrive at the bankruptcy court early on the day you file your petition. This way if there are problems with your petition they can be fixed long before the bankruptcy clerk's office closes for the day. (You should call the bankruptcy court at least one day before you file to make sure the court will be open.)

(2) Bring blank copies of the petition and other forms in case you've made mistakes. Do not assume the bankruptcy court will have blank forms for your convenience.

(3) Have everything in order and ready for filing. If you've done your homework, are prepared, and arrive when the clerk's office opens, your filing can probably be accomplished in a few minutes.

(4) Immediately contact your creditors and tell them that you've filed bankruptcy.

■ After You File

(1) If you are required to file a statement of intention, you must do so within 30 days of your bankruptcy filing or on or before the day of your 341 meeting, whichever comes first. Remember: You must serve a copy of your statement of intention on your Chapter 7 trustee and the creditors listed in the statement of intention.

(2) You will receive notice from the bankruptcy court that you must appear before your creditors to be examined about your financial affairs. As I said in Chapter Three, most of your creditors will not appear at this "341 meeting." The 341 meeting will occur within 20 to 40 days of your petition date.

(3) Within 30 days after the 341 meeting (or of the filing of any amendment or supplement to your schedules) your trustee or any of your creditors may object to your exemptions. If this happens, *you need a lawyer*.

(4) Within 60 days after the 341 meeting, a creditor, your Chapter 7 trustee, or the United States Trustee may object to your discharge. If this happens, *you need a lawyer*.

(5) Once the deadline for filing objections to your discharge has passed (about 120 days after your petition date), you will receive a discharge unless one of the following things has occurred:

- a complaint objecting to your discharge has been filed;

- you have filed a waiver of discharge; or

- the United States Trustee or the bankruptcy court has filed a motion to dismiss your case for *substantial abuse* of the bankruptcy system. (You commit substantial abuse of the system if your debts are primarily consumer debts and you are capable of paying them when due, but you file bankruptcy to avoid payment.)

CHAPTER ELEVEN

Alternatives to Bankruptcy

I hope it is clear to you that bankruptcy should be a last resort solution to your debt problems. I am always upset when I hear about people who file bankruptcy for temporary relief of financial difficulty. Remember: Bankruptcy will provide you only with temporary relief if you cannot use it to discharge your debts. You know that bankruptcy cannot eliminate certain debts (such as student loans, certain tax debts, support obligations, etc.), and, if these types of debts are causing your financial problems, bankruptcy is not the answer for you.

You can obtain help from another quarter: **The National Foundation for Consumer Credit, Inc.**, 8611 Second Avenue, Silver Spring, Maryland 20910. The National Foundation for Consumer Credit, Inc., is the umbrella organization for the Consumer Credit Counseling Services (CCCS) across the nation. There is at least one CCCS in each state. To find the CCCS near you, call 1-800-388-CCCS.

CCCS are non-profit organizations providing a variety of services to people with debt problems, including debt counseling, consolidation and management; and budget planning. (They will also handle your bankruptcy case, if bankruptcy becomes necessary. They charge far less for this service than most lawyers—around $400. Indeed, this savings alone is reason enough for you to contact a CCCS.) Your CCCS can also provide information about debt collection and credit bureau reporting practices. These services are offered at a nominal fee (about $30 per year).

At your initial consultation with your CCCS you will describe your financial situation in detail to a CCCS counselor. This meeting is confidential. (If you are married you will probably be required to attend the meeting with your spouse.) Your counselor will review your financial situation and develop a debt management program for you. You will also be required to destroy your credit cards. (This step is so difficult for some debtors that they ask the counselor or someone else to do it for them!) Your CCCS will contact your creditors to make arrangements with them to restructure your debts. In most cases creditors will agree to lower interest rates on debts and/or stretch out payment terms.

EXAMPLE

Jim owes ABC Bank $2,000 on his ABC Bank Credit Card and is behind on his monthly payments. The credit card carries an interest rate of 19.8%. Jim goes to his local CCCS for help. His CCCS counselor contacts ABC Bank and renegotiates his debt. The counselor gets ABC Bank to agree to lower its interest rate to 9% on Jim's debt. The lower interest rate means Jim's monthly minimum payments on the debt will be sharply reduced.

Once agreements have been reached with most or all of your creditors, you will be responsible for one monthly payment on your debts. You pay this money directly to your CCCS, and your CCCS pays your creditors.

Participation in a CCCS program usually stops creditors from demanding payments. (If your creditors continue to pester you, your CCCS will talk to them for you.) Creditors' concerns about your debts are addressed to your CCCS. Creditors are usually happy to work with debtors in CCCS programs because CCCS payments are timely and payments through a CCCS plan are usually far greater than what creditors receive when debtors file bankruptcy.

Working with creditors through a CCCS plan is a good way to "repair" your credit. Your CCCS may be able to convince your creditors to remove negative financial information from your credit reports in exchange for payments. For example, you might offer a creditor 100% payment if he agrees to tell the credit reporting agencies to delete negative information concerning your dealings with him. The more money you offer a creditor the greater the incentive to work with you. It's best to work with a creditor early on, if you can, than to wait until the creditor has turned your debt over to a collection agency because, as you know, collection agencies are not known for their gentleness towards debtors.

The duration of your CCCS debt management program will depend on several factors: the amount of your debts; willingness of your creditors to renegotiate your debts; amount of debt payments you can comfortably make; and unforeseen financial crises.

A CCCS debt management program is usually better for people than bankruptcy. The trick to making the most of CCCS services is to consult your local CCCS *before* your financial problems reach the emergency stage.

I have visited the CCCS office in New York City, Budget and Credit Counseling Services, Inc., and interviewed its administrators. These people, led by the tireless Luther Gatling, are sincerely dedicated to helping you and people like you solve debt problems. They and their colleagues throughout the nation often work miracles. Call them now!

Appendix A:

Official Bankruptcy Forms

B1
(Rev. 5/92)

FORM 1. VOLUNTARY PETITION

United States Bankruptcy Court	**VOLUNTARY PETITION**
_____ **District of** _____	

IN RE (Name of debtor—If individual, enter: Last, First, Middle)	NAME OF JOINT DEBTOR (Spouse) (Last, First, Middle)
ALL OTHER NAMES used by the debtor in the last 6 years (Include married, maiden, and trade names.)	ALL OTHER NAMES used by the joint debtor in the last 6 years (Include married, maiden, and trade names.)
SOC. SEC./TAX I.D. NO. (If more than one, state all.)	SOC. SEC./TAX I.D. NO. (If more than one, state all.)
STREET ADDRESS OF DEBTOR (No. and street, city, state, and zip code)	STREET ADDRESS OF JOINT DEBTOR (No. and street, city, state, and zip code)
COUNTY OF RESIDENCE OR PRINCIPAL PLACE OF BUSINESS	COUNTY OF RESIDENCE OR PRINCIPAL PLACE OF BUSINESS
MAILING ADDRESS OF DEBTOR (If different from street address)	MAILING ADDRESS OF JOINT DEBTOR (If different from street address)
LOCATION OF PRINCIPAL ASSETS OF BUSINESS DEBTOR (If different from addresses listed above)	VENUE (Check one box) ☐ Debtor has been domiciled or has had a residence, principal place of business, or principal assets in this District for 180 days immediately preceding the date of this petition or for a longer part of such 180 days than in any other District. ☐ There is a bankruptcy case concerning debtor's affiliate, general partner, or partnership pending in this District.

INFORMATION REGARDING DEBTOR (Check applicable boxes)

TYPE OF DEBTOR
☐ Individual
☐ Joint (Husband & Wife)
☐ Partnership
☐ Other: _____
☐ Corporation Publicly Held
☐ Corporation Not Publicly Held
☐ Municipality

CHAPTER OR SECTION OF BANKRUPTCY CODE UNDER WHICH THE PETITION IS FILED (Check one box)
☐ Chapter 7   ☐ Chapter 11   ☐ Chapter 13
☐ Chapter 9   ☐ Chapter 12   ☐ Sec. 304—Case Ancillary to Foreign Proceeding

NATURE OF DEBT
☐ Non-Business/Consumer   ☐ Business—Complete A & B below

FILING FEE (Check one box)
☐ Filing fee attached
☐ Filing fee to be paid in installments. (Applicable to individuals only.) Must attach signed application for the court's consideration certifying that the debtor is unable to pay fee except in installments. Rule 1006(b); see Official Form No. 3.

A. TYPE OF BUSINESS (Check one box)
☐ Farming
☐ Professional
☐ Retail/Wholesale
☐ Railroad
☐ Transportation
☐ Manufacturing/ Mining
☐ Stockbroker
☐ Commodity Broker
☐ Construction
☐ Real Estate
☐ Other Business

NAME AND ADDRESS OF LAW FIRM OR ATTORNEY

B. BRIEFLY DESCRIBE NATURE OF BUSINESS

Telephone No.

NAME(S) OF ATTORNEY(S) DESIGNATED TO REPRESENT THE DEBTOR (Print or Type Names)

☐ Debtor is not represented by an attorney. Telephone No. of Debtor not represented by an attorney: (   )

STATISTICAL/ADMINISTRATIVE INFORMATION (28 U.S.C. § 604)
(Estimates only) (Check applicable boxes)

THIS SPACE FOR COURT USE ONLY

☐ Debtor estimates that funds will be available for distribution to unsecured creditors.
☐ Debtor estimates that, after any exempt property is excluded and administrative expenses paid, there will be no funds available for distribution to unsecured creditors.

ESTIMATED NUMBER OF CREDITORS

1-15	16-49	50-99	100-199	200-999	1000-over
☐	☐	☐	☐	☐	☐

ESTIMATED ASSETS (in thousands of dollars)

Under 50	50-99	100-499	500-999	1000-9999	10,000-99,000	100,000-over
☐	☐	☐	☐	☐	☐	☐

ESTIMATED LIABILITIES (in thousands of dollars)

Under 50	50-99	100-499	500-999	1000-9999	10,000-99,000	100,000-over
☐	☐	☐	☐	☐	☐	☐

EST. NO. OF EMPLOYEES—CH. 11 & 12 ONLY

0	1-19	20-99	100-999	1000-over
☐	☐	☐	☐	☐

EST. NO. OF EQUITY SECURITY HOLDERS—CH. 11 & 12 ONLY

0	1-19	20-99	100-499	500-Over
☐	☐	☐	☐	☐

Bankruptcy Petition

Name of Debtor _____

Case No. _____

(Court use only)

FILING OF PLAN

For Chapter 9, 11, 12 and 13 cases only. Check appropriate box.

☐ A copy of debtor's proposed plan dated _____ is attached.

☐ Debtor intends to file a plan within the time allowed by statute, rule, or order of the court.

PRIOR BANKRUPTCY CASE FILED WITHIN LAST 6 YEARS (If more than one, attach additional sheet)

Location Where Filed	Case Number	Date Filed

PENDING BANKRUPTCY CASE FILED BY ANY SPOUSE, PARTNER, OR AFFILIATE OF THIS DEBTOR (If more than one, attach additional sheet.)

Name of Debtor	Case Number	Date
Relationship	District	Judge

REQUEST FOR RELIEF

Debtor requests relief in accordance with the chapter of title II, United States Code, specified in this petition.

SIGNATURES

ATTORNEY

X _____   _____
Signature   Date

INDIVIDUAL/JOINT DEBTOR(S)	CORPORATE OR PARTNERSHIP DEBTOR
I declare under penalty of perjury that the information provided in this petition is true and correct.	I declare under penalty of perjury that the information provided in this petition is true and correct, and that the filing of this petition on behalf of the debtor has been authorized.
X _____ Signature of Debtor	X _____ Signature of Authorized Individual
Date _____	Print or Type Name of Authorized Individual
X _____ Signature of Joint Debtor	Title of Individual Authorized by Debtor to File this Petition
Date _____	Date

EXHIBIT "A" (To be completed if debtor is a corporation requesting relief under chapter 11.)

☐ Exhibit "A" is attached and made a part of this petition.

TO BE COMPLETED BY INDIVIDUAL CHAPTER 7 DEBTOR WITH PRIMARILY CONSUMER DEBTS (See P.L. 98-353 § 322)

I am aware that I may proceed under chapter 7, 11, or 12, or 13 of title 11, United States Code, understand the relief available under each such chapter, and choose to proceed under chapter 7 of such title.

If I am represented by an attorney, exhibit 'B' has been completed.

X _____   _____
Signature of Debtor   Date

X _____   _____
Signature of Joint Debtor   Date

EXHIBIT "B" (To be completed by attorney for individual chapter 7 debtor(s) with primarily consumer debts.)

I, the attorney for the debtor(s) named in the foregoing petition, declare that I have informed the debtor(s) that (he, she, or they) may proceed under chapter 7, 11, 12, or 13 of title 11, United States Code, and have explained the relief available under each such chapter.

X _____   _____
Signature of Attorney   Date

Bankruptcy Petition, continued

Form 3.   APPLICATION AND ORDER TO PAY FILING FEE IN INSTALLMENTS

[Caption as in Form 16B.]

APPLICATION TO PAY FILING FEES IN INSTALLMENTS

In accordance with Fed. R. Bankr. P. 1006, application is made for permission to pay the filing fee on the following terms:

$ _____ with the filing of the petition, and the balance of

$ _____ in ____ installments, as follows:

    $ _____ on or before _____

    $ _____ on or before _____

    $ _____ on or before _____

    $ _____ on or before _____

I certify that I am unable to pay the filing fee except in installments. I further certify that I have not paid any money or transferred any property to an attorney or any other person for services in connection with this case or in connection with any other pending bankruptcy case and that I will not make any payment or transfer any property for services in connection with the case until the filing fee is paid in full.

Date: _____   _____
                                                Applicant

                                                _____
                                                Address of Applicant

                                                  _____

ORDER

IT IS ORDERED that the debtor pay the filing fee in installments on the terms set forth in the foregoing application.

IT IS FURTHER ORDERED that until the filing fee is paid in full the debtor shall not pay, and no person shall accept, any money for services in connection with this case, and the debtor shall not relinquish, and no person shall accept, any property as payment for services in connection with this case.

BY THE COURT.

Date: _____   _____

Application to Pay Filing Fee in Installments

Form B4
11/92

Form 4. LIST OF CREDITORS HOLDING 20 LARGEST UNSECURED CLAIMS

[Caption as in Form 16B]

LIST OF CREDITORS HOLDING 20 LARGEST UNSECURED CLAIMS

Following is the list of the debtor's creditors holding the 20 largest unsecured claims. The list is prepared in accordance with Fed. R. Bankr. P. 1007(d) for filing in this chapter 11 *[or chapter 9]* case. The list does not include (1) persons who come within the definition of "insider" set forth in 11 U.S.C. § 101, or (2) secured creditors unless the value of the collateral is such that the unsecured deficiency places the creditor among the holders of the 20 largest unsecured claims.

(1)	(2)	(3)	(4)	(5)
Name of creditor and complete mailing address including zip code	*Name, telephone number and complete mailing address, including zip code, of employee, agent, or department of creditor familiar with claim who may be contacted*	*Nature of claim (trade debt, bank loan, government contract, etc.)*	*Indicate if claim is contingent, unliquidated, disputed or subject to setoff*	*Amount of claim [if secured also state value of security]*

Date: _____

_____
Debtor

[Declaration as in Form 2]

List of Creditors Holding 20 Largest Unsecured Claims

Form B6
(6/90

FORM 6. SCHEDULES

Summary of Schedules

Schedule A—Real Property

Schedule B—Personal Property

Schedule C—Property Claimed as Exempt

Schedule D—Creditors Holding Secured Claims

Schedule E—Creditors Holding Unsecured Priority Claims

Schedule F—Creditors Holding Unsecured Nonpriority Claims

Schedule G—Executory Contracts and Unexpired Leases

Schedule H—Codebtors

Schedule I—Current Income of Individual Debtor(s)

Schedule J—Current Expenditures of Individual Debtor(s)

Unsworn Declaration under Penalty of Perjury

GENERAL INSTRUCTIONS: The first page of the debtor's schedules and the first page of any amendments thereto must contain a caption as in Form 16B. Subsequent pages should be identified with the debtor's name and case number. If the schedules are filed with the petition, the case number should be left blank.

Schedules D, E, and F have been designed for the listing of each claim only once. Even when a claim is secured only in part or entitled to priority only in part, it still should be listed only once. A claim which is secured in whole or in part should be listed on Schedule D only, and a claim which is entitled to priority in whole or in part should be listed on Schedule E only. Do not list the same claim twice. If a creditor has more than one claim, such as claims arising from separate transactions, each claim should be scheduled separately.

Review the specific instructions for each schedule before completing the schedule.

Summary of Schedules

FORM B6—Cont
(6/90)

United States Bankruptcy Court

——————————————District of——————————————

In re ——————————————————,   Case No. ————————————————

              Debtor   (If known)

SUMMARY OF SCHEDULES

Indicate as to each schedule whether that schedule is attached and state the number of pages in each. Report the totals from Schedules A, B, D, E, F, I, and J in the boxes provided. Add the amounts from Schedules A and B to determine the total amount of the debtor's assets. Add the amounts from Schedules D, E, and F to determine the total amount of the debtor's liabilities.

NAME OF SCHEDULE	ATTACHED (YES/NO)	NO. OF SHEETS	AMOUNTS SCHEDULED		
			ASSETS	LIABILITIES	OTHER
A— Real Property			$		
B— Personal Property			$		
C— Property Claimed as Exempt					
D— Creditors Holding Secured Claims				$	
E— Creditors Holding Unsecured Priority Claims				$	
F— Creditors Holding Unsecured Nonpriority Claims				$	
G— Executory Contracts and Unexpired Leases					
H— Codebtors					
I— Current Income of Individual Debtor(s)					$
J— Current Expenditures of Individual Debtor(s)					$

Total Number of Sheets
of ALL Schedules ▶ [ ]

Total Assets ▶ $ [ ]

Total Liabilities ▶ $ [ ]

Summary of Schedules, continued

FORM B6A
(10/89)

In re _____ ,   Case No. _____

Debtor   (If known)

SCHEDULE A—REAL PROPERTY

Except as directed below, list all real property in which the debtor has any legal, equitable, or future interest, including all property owned as a co-tenant, community property, or in which the debtor has a life estate. Include any property in which the debtor holds rights and powers exercisable for the debtor's own benefit. If the debtor is married, state whether husband, wife, or both own the property by placing an "H," "W," "J," or "C" in the column labeled "Husband, Wife, Joint, or Community." If the debtor holds no interest in real property, write "None" under "Description and Location of Property."

Do not include interests in executory contracts and unexpired leases on this schedule. List them in Schedule G—Executory Contracts and Unexpired Leases.

If an entity claims to have a lien or hold a secured interest in any property, state the amount of the secured claim. See Schedule D. If no entity claims to hold a secured interest in the property, write "None" in the column labeled "Amount of Secured Claim."

If the debtor is an individual or if a joint petition is filed, state the amount of any exemption claimed in the property only in Schedule C—Property Claimed as Exempt.

DESCRIPTION AND LOCATION OF PROPERTY	NATURE OF DEBTOR'S INTEREST IN PROPERTY	HUSBAND, WIFE, JOINT, OR COMMUNITY	CURRENT MARKET VALUE OF DEBTOR'S INTEREST IN PROPERTY, WITHOUT DEDUCTING ANY SECURED CLAIM OR EXEMPTION	AMOUNT OF SECURED CLAIM

Total ▶ $

(Report also on Summary of Schedules.)

Schedule A: Real Property

In re _____ ,   Case No. _____
                  Debtor   (If known)

SCHEDULE B—PERSONAL PROPERTY

Except as directed below, list all personal property of the debtor of whatever kind. If the debtor has no property in one or more of the categories, place an "x" in the appropriate position in the column labeled "None." If additional space is needed in any category, attach a separate sheet properly identified with the case name, case number, and the number of the category. If the debtor is married, state whether husband, wife, or both own the property by placing an "H," "W," "J," or "C" in the column labeled "Husband, Wife, Joint, or Community." If the debtor is an individual or a joint petition is filed, state the amount of any exemptions claimed only in Schedule C—Property Claimed as Exempt.

Do not list interests in executory contracts and unexpired leases on this schedule. List them in Schedule G—Executory Contracts and Unexpired Leases.

If the property is being held for the debtor by someone else, state that person's name and address under "Description and Location of Property."

TYPE OF PROPERTY	N O N E	DESCRIPTION AND LOCATION OF PROPERTY	HUSBAND, WIFE, JOINT, OR COMMUNITY	CURRENT MARKET VALUE OF DEBTOR'S INTEREST IN PROPERTY, WITH- OUT DEDUCTING ANY SECURED CLAIM OR EXEMPTION
1. Cash on hand.				
2. Checking, savings or other financial accounts, certificates of deposit, or shares in banks, savings and loan, thrift, building and loan, and homestead associations, or credit unions, brokerage houses, or cooperatives.				
3. Security deposits with public utilities, telephone companies, landlords, and others.				
4. Household goods and furnishings, including audio, video, and computer equipment.				
5. Books; pictures and other art objects; antiques; stamp, coin, record, tape, compact disc, and other collections or collectibles.				
6. Wearing apparel.				
7. Furs and jewelry.				
8. Firearms and sports, photographic, and other hobby equipment.				
9. Interests in insurance policies. Name insurance company of each policy and itemize surrender or refund value of each.				
10. Annuities. Itemize and name each issuer.				

Schedule B: Personal Property

FORM B6B—Cont.
(10/89)

In re _____,   Case No. _____
          Debtor   (If known)

SCHEDULE B—PERSONAL PROPERTY
(Continuation Sheet)

TYPE OF PROPERTY	N O N E	DESCRIPTION AND LOCATION OF PROPERTY	HUSBAND, WIFE, JOINT, OR COMMUNITY	CURRENT MARKET VALUE OF DEBTOR'S INTEREST IN PROPERTY, WITHOUT DEDUCTING ANY SECURED CLAIM OR EXEMPTION
11. Interests in IRA, ERISA, Keogh, or other pension or profit sharing plans. Itemize.				
12. Stock and interests in incorporated and unincorporated businesses. Itemize.				
13. Interests in partnerships or joint ventures. Itemize.				
14. Government and corporate bonds and other negotiable and non-negotiable instruments.				
15. Accounts receivable.				
16. Alimony, maintenance, support, and property settlements to which the debtor is or may be entitled. Give particulars.				
17. Other liquidated debts owing debtor including tax refunds. Give particulars.				
18. Equitable or future interests, life estates, and rights or powers exercisable for the benefit of the debtor other than those listed in Schedule of Real Property.				
19. Contingent and noncontingent interests in estate of a decedent, death benefit plan, life insurance policy, or trust.				
20. Other contingent and unliquidated claims of every nature, including tax refunds, counterclaims of the debtor, and rights to setoff claims. Give estimated value of each.				
21. Patents, copyrights, and other intellectual property. Give particulars.				
22. Licenses, franchises, and other general intangibles. Give particulars.				

Schedule B: Personal Property, continued

In re _____ ,   Case No. _____
　　　　　　Debtor　　　　　　　　　　　　　　　　　(If known)

SCHEDULE B—PERSONAL PROPERTY
(Continuation Sheet)

TYPE OF PROPERTY	N O N E	DESCRIPTION AND LOCATION OF PROPERTY	HUSBAND, WIFE, JOINT, OR COMMUNITY	CURRENT MARKET VALUE OF DEBTOR'S INTEREST IN PROPERTY, WITHOUT DEDUCTING ANY SECURED CLAIM OR EXEMPTION
23. Automobiles, trucks, trailers, and other vehicles and accessories.				
24. Boats, motors, and accessories.				
25. Aircraft and accessories.				
26. Office equipment, furnishings, and supplies.				
27. Machinery, fixtures, equipment, and supplies used in business.				
28. Inventory.				
29. Animals.				
30. Crops—growing or harvested. Give particulars.				
31. Farming equipment and implements.				
32. Farm supplies, chemicals, and feed.				
33. Other personal property of any kind not already listed. Itemize.				

_____ continuation sheets attached   Total ▶ | $

(Include amounts from any continuation sheets attached. Report total also on Summary of Schedules.)

Schedule B: Personal Property, continued

FORM B6C
(6/90)

In re _____ ,   Case No. _____
                            Debtor   (If known)

SCHEDULE C—PROPERTY CLAIMED AS EXEMPT

Debtor elects the exemptions to which debtor is entitled under:

(Check one box)

☐ 11 U.S.C. § 522(b)(1): Exemptions provided in 11 U.S.C. § 522(d). Note: These exemptions are available only in certain states.

☐ 11 U.S.C. § 522(b)(2): Exemptions available under applicable nonbankruptcy federal laws, state or local law where the debtor's domicile has been located for the 180 days immediately preceding the filing of the petition, or for a longer portion of the 180-day period than in any other place, and the debtor's interest as a tenant by the entirety or joint tenant to the extent the interest is exempt from process under applicable nonbankruptcy law.

DESCRIPTION OF PROPERTY	SPECIFY LAW PROVIDING EACH EXEMPTION	VALUE OF CLAIMED EXEMPTION	CURRENT MARKET VALUE OF PROPERTY WITHOUT DEDUCTING EXEMPTION

Schedule C: Property Claimed as Exempt

FORM B6D
(6/90)

In re _____, Case No. _____
                  Debtor   (If known)

SCHEDULE D—CREDITORS HOLDING SECURED CLAIMS

State the name, mailing address, including zip code, and account number, if any, of all entities holding claims secured by property of the debtor as of the date of filing of the petition. List creditors holding all types of secured interests such as judgment liens, garnishments, statutory liens, mortgages, deeds of trust, and other security interests. List creditors in alphabetical order to the extent practicable. If all secured creditors will not fit on this page, use the continuation sheet provided.

If any entity other than a spouse in a joint case may be jointly liable on a claim, place an "X" in the column labeled "Codebtor," include the entity on the appropriate schedule of creditors, and complete Schedule H—Codebtors. If a joint petition is filed, state whether husband, wife, both of them, or the marital community may be liable on each claim by placing an "H," "W," "J," or "C" in the column labeled "Husband, Wife, Joint, or Community."

If the claim is contingent, place an "X" in the column labeled "Contingent." If the claim is unliquidated, place an "X" in the column labeled "Unliquidated." If the claim is disputed, place an "X" in the column labeled "Disputed." (You may need to place an "X" in more than one of these three columns.)

Report the total of all claims listed on this schedule in the box labeled "Total" on the last sheet of the completed schedule. Report this total also on the Summary of Schedules.

☐ Check this box if debtor has no creditors holding secured claims to report on this Schedule D.

CREDITOR'S NAME AND MAILING ADDRESS INCLUDING ZIP CODE	CODEBTOR	HUSBAND, WIFE, JOINT, OR COMMUNITY	DATE CLAIM WAS INCURRED, NATURE OF LIEN, AND DESCRIPTION AND MARKET VALUE OF PROPERTY SUBJECT TO LIEN	CONTINGENT	UNLIQUIDATED	DISPUTED	AMOUNT OF CLAIM WITHOUT DEDUCTING VALUE OF COLLATERAL	UNSECURED PORTION, IF ANY
ACCOUNT NO.								
			VALUE $					
ACCOUNT NO.								
			VALUE $					
ACCOUNT NO.								
			VALUE $					
ACCOUNT NO.								
			VALUE $					

_____ continuation sheets attached

Subtotal ▶ $ _____
(Total of this page)
Total ▶ $ _____
(Use only on last page)
(Report total also on Summary of Schedules)

Schedule D: Creditors Holding Secured Claims

FORM B6D—Cont.
(10/89)

In re _____ ,   Case No. _____
　　　　　　　　　　Debtor　　　　　　　　　　　　　　　　　　　　　　　(If known)

SCHEDULE D—CREDITORS HOLDING SECURED CLAIMS
(Continuation Sheet)

CREDITOR'S NAME AND MAILING ADDRESS INCLUDING ZIP CODE	CODEBTOR	HUSBAND, WIFE, JOINT, OR COMMUNITY	DATE CLAIM WAS INCURRED, NATURE OF LIEN, AND DESCRIPTION AND MARKET VALUE OF PROPERTY SUBJECT TO LIEN	CONTINGENT	UNLIQUIDATED	DISPUTED	AMOUNT OF CLAIM WITHOUT DEDUCTING VALUE OF COLLATERAL	UNSECURED PORTION, IF ANY
ACCOUNT NO.								
			VALUE $					
ACCOUNT NO.								
			VALUE $					
ACCOUNT NO.								
			VALUE $					
ACCOUNT NO.								
			VALUE $					
ACCOUNT NO.								
			VALUE $					

Sheet no. _____ of _____ continuation sheets attached to Schedule of Creditors Holding Secured Claims   Subtotal ▶ $

(Total of this page)

Total ▶ $

(Use only on last page)

(Report total also on Summary of Schedules)

Schedule D: Creditors Holding Secured Claims, continued

FORM B6E
(6/92)

In Re _____.   Case No. _____.
                Debtor   (if known)

SCHEDULE E - CREDITORS HOLDING UNSECURED PRIORITY CLAIMS

A complete list of claims entitled to priority, listed separately by type of priority, is to be set forth on the sheets provided. Only holders of unsecured claims entitled to priority should be listed in this schedule. In the boxes provided on the attached sheets, state the name and mailing address, including zip code, and account number, if any, of all entities holding priority claims against the debtor or the property of the debtor, as of the date of the filing of the petition.

If any entity other than a spouse in a joint case may be jointly liable on a claim, place an "X" in the column labeled "Codebtor," include the entity on the appropriate schedule of creditor, and complete Schedule H-Codebtors. If a joint petition is filed, state whether husband, wife, both of them or the marital community may be liable on each claim by placing an "H,""W","J", or "C" in the column labeled "Husband, Wife, Joint, or Community."

If the claim is contingent, place an "X" in the column labeled "Contingent." If the claim is unliquidated place an "X" in the column labeled "Unliquidated." If the claim is disputed, place an "X" in the column labeled "Disputed." (You may need to place an "X" in more than one of these three columns.)

Report the total of claims listed on each sheet in the box labeled, "Subtotal" on each sheet. Report the total of all claims listed on this Schedule E in the box labeled "Total" on the last sheet of the completed schedule. Repeat this total also on the Summary of Schedules.

☐ Check this box if debtor has no creditors holding unsecured priority claims to report on this Schedule E.

TYPES OF PRIORITY CLAIMS (Check the appropriate box(es) below if claims in that category are listed on the attached sheets)

☐ Extensions of credit in an involuntary case

Claims arising in the ordinary course of the debtor's business or financial affairs after the commencement of the case but before the earlier of the appointment of a trustee or the order for relief. 11 U.S.C. § 507(a)(2).

☐ Wages, salaries, and commissions

Wages salaries, and commissions, including vacation, severance, and sick leave pay owing to employees up to a maximum of $2000 per employee, earned within 90 days immediately preceding the filing of the original petition, or the cessation of business, whichever occurred first, to the extent provided in 11 U.S.C. § 507(a)(3).

☐ Contributions to employee benefit plans

Money owed to employee benefit plans for services rendered within 180 days immediately preceding the filing of the original petition, or the cessation of business, whichever occurred first, to the extent provided in 11 U.S.C. § 507(a)(4).

☐ Certain farmers and fishermen

Claims of certain farmers and fishermen, up to a maximum of $2000 per farmer or fisherman, against the debtor, as provided in 11 U.S.C. § 507(a)(5).

☐ Deposits by individuals

Claims of individuals up to a maximum of $900 for deposits for the purchase, lease, or rental of property or services for personal, family, or household use, that were not delivered or provided. 11 U.S.C. § 507(a)(6).

☐ Taxes and Certain Other Debts Owed to Governmental Units

Taxes, customs duties, and penalties owing to federal, state, and local governmental units as set forth in 11 U.S.C. § 507(a)(7).

☐ Commitments to Maintain the Capital of an Insured Depository Institution

Claims based on commitments to the FDIC, RTC, Director of the Office of Thrift Supervision, Comptroller of the Currency, or Board of Governors of the Federal Reserve System, or their predecessors or successors, to maintain the capital of an insured depository institution. 11 U.S.C. § 507 (a)(8).

_____ continuation sheets attached

Schedule E: Creditors Holding Unsecured Priority Claims

FORM B6E—Cont.
(10/89)

In re _____,   Case No. _____

Debtor   (If known)

SCHEDULE E—CREDITORS, HOLDING UNSECURED PRIORITY CLAIMS
(Continuation Sheet)

TYPE OF PRIORITY _____

CREDITOR'S NAME AND MAILING ADDRESS INCLUDING ZIP CODE	CODEBTOR	HUSBAND, WIFE, JOINT, OR COMMUNITY	DATE CLAIM WAS INCURRED AND CONSIDERATION FOR CLAIM	CONTINGENT	UNLIQUIDATED	DISPUTED	TOTAL AMOUNT OF CLAIM	AMOUNT ENTITLED TO PRIORITY
ACCOUNT NO.								
ACCOUNT NO.								
ACCOUNT NO.								
ACCOUNT NO.								
ACCOUNT NO.								

Sheet no. _____ of _____ sheets attached to Schedule of Creditors
Holding Priority Claims

Subtotal ▶ $ _____
(Total of this page)

Total ▶ $ _____
(Use only on last page of the completed Schedule E.)
(Report total also on Summary of Schedules)

Schedule E: Creditors Holding Unsecured Priority Claims, continued

FORM B6F
(10/89)

In re _____,   Case No. _____
                    Debtor   (If known)

SCHEDULE F—CREDITORS HOLDING UNSECURED NONPRIORITY CLAIMS

State the name, mailing address, including zip code, and account number, if any, of all entities holding unsecured claims without priority against the debtor or the property of the debtor, as of the date of filing of the petition. Do not include claims listed in Schedules D and E. If all creditors will not fit on this page, use the continuation sheet provided.

If any entity other than a spouse in a joint case may be jointly liable on a claim, place an "X" in the column labeled "Codebtor," include the entity on the appropriate schedule of creditors, and complete Schedule H—Codebtors. If a joint petition is filed, state whether husband, wife, both of them, or the marital community maybe liable on each claim by placing an "H," "W," "J," or "C" in the column labeled "Husband, Wife, Joint, or Community."

If the claim is contingent, place an "X" in the column labeled "Contingent." If the claim is unliquidated, place an "X" in the column labeled "Unliquidated." If the claim is disputed, place an "X" in the column labeled "Disputed." (You may need to place an "X" in more than one of these three columns.)

Report total of all claims listed on this schedule in the box labeled "Total" on the last sheet of the completed schedule. Report this total also on the Summary of Schedules.

☐ Check this box if debtor has no creditors holding unsecured non priority claims to report on this Schedule F.

CREDITOR'S NAME AND MAILING ADDRESS INCLUDING ZIP CODE	CODEBTOR	HUSBAND, WIFE, OR JOINT	DATE CLAIM WAS INCURRED AND CONSIDERATION FOR CLAIM. IF CLAIM IS SUBJECT TO SETOFF, SO STATE.	CONTINGENT	UNLIQUIDATED	DISPUTED	AMOUNT OF CLAIM
ACCOUNT NO.							
ACCOUNT NO.							
ACCOUNT NO.							
ACCOUNT NO.							

_____ continuation sheets attached

Subtotal ▶ $ _____

Total ▶ $ _____
(Report total also on Summary of Schedules)

Schedule F: Creditors Holding Unsecured Nonpriority Claims

FORM B6F—Cont.
(10/89)

In re _____,   Case No. _____
_____Debtor_____   (If known)

SCHEDULE F—CREDITORS HOLDING UNSECURED NONPRIORITY CLAIMS
(Continuation Sheet)

CREDITOR'S NAME AND MAILING ADDRESS INCLUDING ZIP CODE	CODEBTOR	HUSBAND, WIFE, JOINT OR COMMUNITY	DATE CLAIM WAS INCURRED AND CONSIDERATION FOR CLAIM. IF CLAIM IS SUBJECT TO SETOFF, SO STATE.	CONTINGENT	UNLIQUIDATED	DISPUTED	AMOUNT OF CLAIM
ACCOUNT NO.							
ACCOUNT NO.							
ACCOUNT NO.							
ACCOUNT NO.							
ACCOUNT NO.							

Sheet no. _____ of _____ sheets attached to Schedule of
Creditors Holding Unsecured Nonpriority Claims

Subtotal ▶ $ _____
(Total of this page)
Total ▶ $ _____
(Use only on last page of the completed Schedule E.)
(Report total also on Summary of Schedule)

Schedule F: Creditors Holding Unsecured Nonpriority Claims, continued

FORM B6G
(10/89)

In re _____ ,   Case No. _____
                    Debtor   (If known)

SCHEDULE G—EXECUTORY CONTRACTS AND UNEXPIRED LEASES

Describe all executory contracts of any nature and all unexpired leases of real or personal property. Include any timeshare interests.

State nature of debtor's interest in contract, i.e., "Purchaser," "Agent," etc. State whether debtor is the lessor or lessee of a lease.

Provide the names and complete mailing addresses of all other parties to each lease or contract described.

NOTE: A party listed on this schedule will not receive notice of the filing of this case unless the party is also scheduled in the appropriate schedule of creditors.

☐ Check this box if debtor has no executory contracts or unexpired leases.

NAME AND MAILING ADDRESS, INCLUDING ZIP CODE, OF OTHER PARTIES TO LEASE OR CONTRACT.	DESCRIPTION OF CONTRACT OR LEASE AND NATURE OF DEBTOR'S INTEREST. STATE WHETHER LEASE IS FOR NONRESIDENTIAL REAL PROPERTY. STATE CONTRACT NUMBER OF ANY GOVERNMENT CONTRACT.

Schedule G: Executory Contracts and Unexpired Leases

FORM B6H
(6/90)

In re _____ ,   Case No. _____
                    Debtor   (If known)

SCHEDULE H—CODEBTORS

Provide the information requested concerning any person or entity, other than a spouse in a joint case, that is also liable on any debts listed by debtor in the schedules of creditors. Include all guarantors and co-signers. In community property states, a married debtor not filing a joint case should report the name and address of the nondebtor spouse on this schedule. Include all names used by the nondebtor spouse during the six years immediately preceding the commencement of this case.

☐ Check this box if debtor has no codebtors.

NAME AND ADDRESS OF CODEBTOR	NAME AND ADDRESS OF CREDITOR

Schedule H: Codebtors

FORM B6I
(6/90)

In re _____,   Case No. _____
         Debtor   (If known)

SCHEDULE I—CURRENT INCOME OF INDIVIDUAL DEBTOR(S)

The column labeled "Spouse" must be completed in all cases filed by joint debtors and by a married debtor in a chapter 12 or 13 case whether or not a joint petition is filed, unless the spouses are separated and a joint petition is not filed.

Debtor's Marital Status:	DEPENDENTS OF DEBTOR AND SPOUSE		
	NAMES	AGE	RELATIONSHIP

Employment:	DEBTOR	SPOUSE
Occupation		
Name of Employer		
How long employed		
Address of Employer		

Income: (Estimate of average monthly income)	DEBTOR	SPOUSE
Current monthly gross wages, salary, and commissions (pro rate if not paid monthly.)	$ _____	$ _____
Estimated monthly overtime	$ _____	$ _____
SUBTOTAL	$ _____	$ _____
LESS PAYROLL DEDUCTIONS		
a. Payroll taxes and social security	$ _____	$ _____
b. Insurance	$ _____	$ _____
c. Union dues	$ _____	$ _____
d. Other (Specify: _____)	$ _____	$ _____
SUBTOTAL OF PAYROLL DEDUCTIONS	$ _____	$ _____
TOTAL NET MONTHLY TAKE HOME PAY	$ _____	$ _____
Regular income from operation of business or profession or farm (attach detailed statement)	$ _____	$ _____
Income from real property	$ _____	$ _____
Interest and dividends	$ _____	$ _____
Alimony, maintenance or support payments payable to the debtor for the debtor's use or that of dependents listed above.	$ _____	$ _____
Social security or other government assistance (Specify) _____	$ _____	$ _____
Pension or retirement income	$ _____	$ _____
Other monthly income (Specify) _____	$ _____	$ _____
	$ _____	$ _____
TOTAL MONTHLY INCOME	$ _____	$ _____

TOTAL COMBINED MONTHLY INCOME $ _____   (Report also on Summary of Schedules)

Describe any increase or decrease of more than 10% in any of the above categories anticipated to occur within the year following the filing of this document:

Schedule I: Current Income of Individual Debtor(s)

FORM B6J
(6/90)

In re _____ ,   Case No. _____
                    Debtor   (If known)

SCHEDULE J—CURRENT EXPENDITURES OF INDIVIDUAL DEBTOR(S)

Complete this schedule by estimating the average monthly expenses of the debtor and the debtor's family. Pro rate any payments made bi-weekly, quarterly, semi-annually, or annually to show monthly rate.

☐ Check this box if a joint petition is filed and debtor's spouse maintains a separate household. Complete a separate schedule of expenditures labeled "Spouse."

Rent or home mortgage payment (include lot rented for mobile home)	$ _____
Are real estate taxes included? Yes _____ No _____	
Is property insurance included? Yes _____ No _____	
Utilities Electricity and heating fuel	$ _____
Water and sewer	$ _____
Telephone	$ _____
Other _____	$ _____
Home maintenance (repairs and upkeep)	$ _____
Food	$ _____
Clothing	$ _____
Laundry and dry cleaning	$ _____
Medical and dental expenses	$ _____
Transportation (not including car payments)	$ _____
Recreation, clubs and entertainment, newspapers, magazines, etc.	$ _____
Charitable contributions	$ _____
Insurance (not deducted from wages or included in home mortgage payments)	
Homeowner's or renter's	$ _____
Life	$ _____
Health	$ _____
Auto	$ _____
Other _____	$ _____
Taxes (not deducted from wages or included in home mortgage payments) (Specify) _____	$ _____
Installment payments: (In chapter 12 and 13 cases, do not list payments to be included in the plan)	
Auto	$ _____
Other _____	$ _____
Other _____	$ _____
Alimony, maintenance, and support paid to others	$ _____
Payments for support of additional dependents not living at your home	$ _____
Regular expenses from operation of business, profession, or farm (attach detailed statement)	$ _____
Other _____	$ _____
TOTAL MONTHLY EXPENSES (Report also on Summary of Schedules)	$ _____

[FOR CHAPTER 12 AND 13 DEBTORS ONLY]
Provide the information requested below, including whether plan payments are to be made bi-weekly, monthly, annually, or at some other regular interval.

A. Total projected monthly income	$ _____
B. Total projected monthly expenses	$ _____
C. Excess income (A minus B)	$ _____
D. Total amount to be paid into plan each _____	$ _____
(interval)	

Schedule J: Current Expenditures of Individual Debtor(s)

FORM B6—Cont.
(6/90)

In re _____,   Case No. _____
           Debtor   (If known)

DECLARATION CONCERNING DEBTOR'S SCHEDULES

DECLARATION UNDER PENALTY OF PERJURY BY INDIVIDUAL DEBTOR

I declare under penalty of perjury that I have read the foregoing summary and schedules, consisting of _____ sheets, and that they are true and correct to the best of my knowledge, information, and belief.   (Total shown on summary page plus 1.)

Date _____   Signature: _____
                                                  Debtor

Date _____   Signature: _____
                                            (Joint Debtor, if any)

                                     [If joint case, both spouses must sign.]

- -

DECLARATION UNDER PENALTY OF PERJURY ON BEHALF OF CORPORATION OR PARTNERSHIP

I, the _____ [the president or other officer or an authorized agent of the corporation or a member or an authorized agent of the partnership] of the _____ [corporation or partnership] named as debtor in this case, declare under penalty of perjury that I have read the foregoing summary and schedules, consisting of _____ sheets, and that they are true and correct to the best of my knowledge, information, and belief.   (Total shown on summary page plus 1.)

Date _____

                   Signature: _____

                                   _____
                           [Print or type name of individual signing on behalf of debtor.]

[An individual signing on behalf of a partnership or corporation must indicate position or relationship to debtor.]

- -

Penalty for making a false statement or concealing property: Fine of up to $500,000 or imprisonment for up to 5 years or both. 18 U.S.C. §§ 152 and 3571.

Unsworn Declaration under Penalty of Perjury

B7
(Rev. 12/92)

FORM 7. STATEMENT OF FINANCIAL AFFAIRS

UNITED STATES BANKRUPTCY COURT

————————————— DISTRICT OF —————————————

In re ————————————————— ,   Case No. ———————————
          (Name)   (If known)

Debtor

STATEMENT OF FINANCIAL AFFAIRS

This statement is to be completed by every debtor. Spouses filing a joint petition may file a single statement on which the information for both spouses is combined. If the case is filed under chapter 12 or chapter 13, a married debtor must furnish information for both spouses whether or not a joint petition is filed, unless the spouses are separated and a joint petition is not filed. An individual debtor engaged in business as a sole proprietor, partner, family farmer, or self-employed professional, should provide the information requested on this statement concerning all such activities as well as the individual's personal affairs.

Questions 1-15 are to be completed by all debtors. Debtors that are or have been in business, as defined below, also must complete Questions 16-21. **If the answer to any question is "None," or the question is not applicable, mark the box labeled "None."** If additional space is needed for the answer to any question, use and attach a separate sheet properly identified with the case name, case number (if known), and the number of the question.

DEFINITIONS

"In business." A debtor is "in business" for the purpose of this form if the debtor is a corporation or partnership. An individual debtor is "in business" for the purpose of this form if the debtor is or has been, within the two years immediately preceding the filing of this bankruptcy case, any of the following: an officer, director, managing executive, or person in control of a corporation; a partner, other than a limited partner, of a partnership; a sole proprietor or self-employed.

"Insider." The term "insider" includes but is not limited to: relatives of the debtor; general partners of the debtor and their relatives; corporations of which the debtor is an officer, director, or person in control; officers, directors, and any person in control of a corporate debtor and their relatives; affiliates of the debtor and insiders of such affiliates; any managing agent of the debtor. 11 U.S.C. §101(30).

————————————————————

1. Income from employment or operation of business

None   State the gross amount of income the debtor has received from employment, trade, or profession, or from operation of
☐   the debtor's business from the beginning of this calendar year to the date this case was commenced. State also the gross amounts received during the two years immediately preceding this calendar year. (A debtor that maintains, or has maintained, financial records on the basis of a fiscal rather than a calendar year may report fiscal year income. Identify the beginning and ending dates of the debtor's fiscal year.) If a joint petition is filed, state income for each spouse separately. (Married debtors filing under chapter 12 or chapter 13 must state income of both spouses whether or not a joint petition is filed, unless the spouses are separated and a joint petition is not filed.)

AMOUNT   SOURCE (if more than one)

B7
(Rev. 12/92)

2. **Income other than from employment or operation of business**

None   State the amount of income received by the debtor other than from employment, trade, profession, or operation of
☐   the debtor's business during the **two years** immediately preceding the commencement of this case. Give particulars. If a
         joint petition is filed, state income for each spouse separately. (Married debtors filing under chapter 12 or chapter 13 must
         state income for each spouse whether or not a joint petition is filed, unless the spouses are separated and a joint petition
         is not filed.)

AMOUNT   SOURCE

3. **Payments to creditors**

None   a. List all payments on loans, installment purchases of goods or services, and other debts, aggregating more than $600 to
☐   any creditor, made within **90 days** immediately preceding the commencement of this case. (Married debtors filing under
         chapter 12 or chapter 13 must include payments by either or both spouses whether or not a joint petition is filed, unless
         the spouses are separated and a joint petition is not filed.)

	DATES OF	AMOUNT	AMOUNT
	PAYMENTS	PAID	STILL OWING
NAME AND ADDRESS OF CREDITOR			

None   b. List all payments made within **one year** immediately preceding the commencement of this case to or for the benefit of
☐   creditors who are or were insiders. (Married debtors filing under chapter 12 or chapter 13 must include payments by either
         or both spouses whether or not a joint petition is filed, unless the spouses are separated and a joint petition is not filed.)

| NAME AND ADDRESS OF CREDITOR | DATE OF | AMOUNT | AMOUNT |
| AND RELATIONSHIP TO DEBTOR | PAYMENT | PAID | STILL OWING |

4. **Suits and administrative proceedings, executions, garnishments and attachments**

None   a. List all suits and administrative proceedings to which the debtor is or was a party within **one year** immediately
☐   preceding the filing of this bankruptcy case. (Married debtors filing under chapter 12 or chapter 13 must include
         information concerning either or both spouses whether or not a joint petition is filed, unless the spouses are separated and
         a joint petition is not filed.)

| CAPTION OF SUIT | | COURT OR AGENCY | STATUS OR |
| AND CASE NUMBER | NATURE OF PROCEEDING | AND LOCATION | DISPOSITION |

Statement of Financial Affairs, continued

None ☐ b. Describe all property that has been attached, garnished or seized under any legal or equitable process within **one year** immediately preceding the commencement of this case. (Married debtors filing under chapter 12 or chapter 13 must include information concerning property of either or both spouses whether or not a joint petition is filed, unless the spouses are separated and a joint petition is not filed.)

NAME AND ADDRESS OF PERSON FOR WHOSE BENEFIT PROPERTY WAS SEIZED	DATE OF SEIZURE	DESCRIPTION AND VALUE OF PROPERTY

---

5. Repossessions, foreclosures and returns

None ☐ List all property that has been repossessed by a creditor, sold at a foreclosure sale, transferred through a deed in lieu of foreclosure or returned to the seller, within **one year** immediately preceding the commencement of this case. (Married debtors filing under chapter 12 or chapter 13 must include information concerning property of either or both spouses whether or not a joint petition is filed, unless the spouses are separated and a joint petition is not filed.)

NAME AND ADDRESS OF CREDITOR OR SELLER	DATE OF REPOSSESSION, FORECLOSURE SALE, TRANSFER OR RETURN	DESCRIPTION AND VALUE OF PROPERTY

---

6. Assignments and receiverships

None ☐ a. Describe any assignment of property for the benefit of creditors made within **120 days** immediately preceding the commencement of this case. (Married debtors filing under chapter 12 or chapter 13 must include any assignment by either or both spouses whether or not a joint petition is filed, unless the spouses are separated and a joint petition is not filed.)

NAME AND ADDRESS OF ASSIGNEE	DATE OF ASSIGNMENT	TERMS OF ASSIGNMENT OR SETTLEMENT

None ☐ b. List all property which has been in the hands of a custodian, receiver, or court-appointed official within **one year** immediately preceding the commencement of this case. (Married debtors filing under chapter 12 or chapter 13 must include information concerning property of either or both spouses whether or not a joint petition is filed, unless the spouses are separated and a joint petition is not filed.)

NAME AND ADDRESS OF CUSTODIAN	NAME AND LOCATION OF COURT CASE TITLE & NUMBER	DATE OF ORDER	DESCRIPTION AND VALUE OF PROPERTY

Statement of Financial Affairs, continued

7. Gifts

None ☐   List all gifts or charitable contributions made within **one year** immediately preceding the commencement of this case except ordinary and usual gifts to family members aggregating less than $200 in value per individual family member and charitable contributions aggregating less than $100 per recipient. (Married debtors filing under chapter 12 or chapter 13 must include gifts or contributions by either or both spouses whether or not a joint petition is filed, unless the spouses are separated and a joint petition is not filed.)

NAME AND ADDRESS OF PERSON OR ORGANIZATION	RELATIONSHIP TO DEBTOR, IF ANY	DATE OF GIFT	DESCRIPTION AND VALUE OF GIFT

8. Losses

None ☐   List all losses from fire, theft, other casualty or gambling within **one year** immediately preceding the commencement of this case or **since the commencement of this case.** (Married debtors filing under chapter 12 or chapter 13 must include losses by either or both spouses whether or not a joint petition is filed, unless the spouses are separated and a joint petition is not filed.)

DESCRIPTION AND VALUE OF PROPERTY	DESCRIPTION OF CIRCUMSTANCES AND, IF LOSS WAS COVERED IN WHOLE OR IN PART BY INSURANCE, GIVE PARTICULARS	DATE OF LOSS

9. Payments related to debt counseling or bankruptcy

None ☐   List all payments made or property transferred by or on behalf of the debtor to any persons, including attorneys, for consultation concerning debt consolidation, relief under the bankruptcy law or preparation of a petition in bankruptcy within **one year** immediately preceding the commencement of this case.

NAME AND ADDRESS OF PAYEE	DATE OF PAYMENT, NAME OF PAYOR IF OTHER THAN DEBTOR	AMOUNT OF MONEY OR DESCRIPTION AND VALUE OF PROPERTY

Statement of Financial Affairs, continued

10. Other transfers

None ☐   a. List all other property, other than property transferred in the ordinary course of the business or financial affairs of the debtor, transferred either absolutely or as security within **one year** immediately preceding the commencement of this case. (Married debtors filing under chapter 12 or chapter 13 must include transfers by either or both spouses whether or not a joint petition is filed, unless the spouses are separated and a joint petition is not filed.)

NAME AND ADDRESS OF TRANSFEREE, RELATIONSHIP TO DEBTOR	DATE	DESCRIBE PROPERTY TRANSFERRED AND VALUE RECEIVED

---

11. Closed financial accounts

None ☐   List all financial accounts and instruments held in the name of the debtor or for the benefit of the debtor which were closed, sold, or otherwise transferred within **one year** immediately preceding the commencement of this case. Include checking, savings, or other financial accounts, certificates of deposit, or other instruments; shares and share accounts held in banks, credit unions, pension funds, cooperatives, associations, brokerage houses and other financial institutions. (Married debtors filing under chapter 12 or chapter 13 must include information concerning accounts or instruments held by or for either or both spouses whether or not a joint petition is filed, unless the spouses are separated and a joint petition is not filed.)

NAME AND ADDRESS OF INSTITUTION	TYPE AND NUMBER OF ACCOUNT AND AMOUNT OF FINAL BALANCE	AMOUNT AND DATE OF SALE OR CLOSING

12. Safe deposit boxes

None ☐   List each safe deposit or other box or depository in which the debtor has or had securities, cash, or other valuables within **one year** immediately preceding the commencement of this case. (Married debtors filing under chapter 12 or chapter 13 must include boxes or depositories of either or both spouses whether or not a joint petition is filed, unless the spouses are separated and a joint petition is not filed.)

NAME AND ADDRESS OF BANK OR OTHER DEPOSITORY	NAMES AND ADDRESSES OF THOSE WITH ACCESS TO BOX OR DEPOSITORY	DESCRIPTION OF CONTENTS	DATE OF TRANSFER OR SURRENDER, IF ANY

Statement of Financial Affairs, continued

13. Setoffs

None ☐   List all setoffs made by any creditor, including a bank, against a debt or deposit of the debtor within **90 days** preceding the commencement of this case. (Married debtors filing under chapter 12 or chapter 13 must include information concerning either or both spouses whether or not a joint petition is filed, unless the spouses are separated and a joint petition is not filed.)

NAME AND ADDRESS OF CREDITOR	DATE OF SETOFF	AMOUNT OF SETOFF

---

14. Property held for another person

None ☐   List all property owned by another person that the debtor holds or controls.

NAME AND ADDRESS OF OWNER	DESCRIPTION AND VALUE OF PROPERTY	LOCATION OF PROPERTY

---

15. Prior address of debtor

None ☐   If the debtor has moved within the **two years** immediately preceding the commencement of this case, list all premises which the debtor occupied during that period and vacated prior to the commencement of this case. If a joint petition is filed, report also any separate address of either spouse.

ADDRESS	NAME USED	DATES OF OCCUPANCY

Statement of Financial Affairs, continued

The following questions are to be completed by every debtor that is a corporation or partnership and by any individual debtor who is or has been, within the two years immediately preceding the commencement of this case, any of the following: an officer, director, managing executive, or owner of more than 5 percent of the voting securities of a corporation; a partner, other than a limited partner, of a partnership; a sole proprietor or otherwise self-employed.

(An individual or joint debtor should complete this portion of the statement only if the debtor is or has been in business, as defined above, within the two years immediately preceding the commencement of this case.)

16. Nature, location and name of business

None
☐
a. If the debtor is an individual, list the names and addresses of all businesses in which the debtor was an officer, director, partner, or managing executive of a corporation, partnership, sole proprietorship, or was a self-employed professional within the two years immediately preceding the commencement of this case, or in which the debtor owned 5 percent or more of the voting or equity securities within the two years immediately preceding the commencement of this case.

b. If the debtor is a partnership, list the names and addresses of all businesses in which the debtor was a partner or owned 5 percent or more of the voting securities, within the two years immediately preceding the commencement of this case.

c. If the debtor is a corporation, list the names and addresses of all businesses in which the debtor was a partner or owned 5 percent or more of the voting securities within the two years immediately preceding the commencement of this case.

NAME	ADDRESS	NATURE OF BUSINESS	BEGINNING AND ENDING DATES OF OPERATION

17. Books, records and financial statements

None
☐
a. List all bookkeepers and accountants who within the six years immediately preceding the filing of this bankruptcy case kept or supervised the keeping of books of account and records of the debtor.

NAME AND ADDRESS	DATES SERVICES RENDERED

None
☐
b. List all firms or individuals who within the two years immediately preceding the filing of this bankruptcy case have audited the books of account and records, or prepared a financial statement of the debtor.

NAME	ADDRESS	DATES SERVICES RENDERED

Statement of Financial Affairs, continued

None c. List all firms or individuals who at the time of the commencement of this case were in possession of the books of account and records of the debtor. If any of the books of account and records are not available, explain.

NAME   ADDRESS

None d. List all financial institutions, creditors and other parties, including mercantile and trade agencies, to whom a financial statement was issued within the two years immediately preceding the commencement of this case by the debtor.

NAME AND ADDRESS   DATE ISSUED

18. Inventories

None a. List the dates of the last two inventories taken of your property, the name of the person who supervised the taking of each inventory, and the dollar amount and basis of each inventory.

DOLLAR AMOUNT OF INVENTORY
DATE OF INVENTORY   INVENTORY SUPERVISOR   (Specify cost, market or other basis)

None b. List the name and address of the person having possession of the records of each of the two inventories reported in a., above.

NAME AND ADDRESSES OF CUSTODIAN
DATE OF INVENTORY   OF INVENTORY RECORDS

19. Current Partners, Officers, Directors and Shareholders

None a. If the debtor is a partnership, list the nature and percentage of partnership interest of each member of the partnership.

NAME AND ADDRESS   NATURE OF INTEREST   PERCENTAGE OF INTEREST

Statement of Financial Affairs, continued

None ☐ b. If the debtor is a corporation, list all officers and directors of the corporation, and each stockholder who directly or indirectly owns, controls, or holds 5 percent or more of the voting securities of the corporation.

NAME AND ADDRESS	TITLE	NATURE AND PERCENTAGE OF STOCK OWNERSHIP

20. Former partners, officers, directors and shareholders

None ☐ a. If the debtor is a partnership, list each member who withdrew from the partnership within one year immediately preceding the commencement of this case.

NAME	ADDRESS	DATE OF WITHDRAWAL

None ☐ b. If the debtor is a corporation, list all officers, or directors whose relationship with the corporation terminated within one year immediately preceding the commencement of this case.

NAME AND ADDRESS	TITLE	DATE OF TERMINATION

21. Withdrawals from a partnership or distributions by a corporation

None ☐ If the debtor is a partnership or corporation, list all withdrawals or distributions credited or given to an insider, including compensation in any form, bonuses, loans, stock redemptions, options exercised and any other perquisite during one year immediately preceding the commencement of this case.

NAME & ADDRESS OF RECIPIENT, RELATIONSHIP TO DEBTOR	DATE AND PURPOSE OF WITHDRAWAL	AMOUNT OF MONEY OR DESCRIPTION AND VALUE OF PROPERTY

• • • • • •

Statement of Financial Affairs, continued

[If completed by an individual or individual and spouse]

I declare under penalty of perjury that I have read the answers contained in the foregoing statement of financial affairs and any attachments thereto and that they are true and correct.

Date _____   Signature _____
                                of Debtor

Date _____   Signature _____
                                of Joint Debtor
                                (if any)

• • • • • •

[If completed on behalf of a partnership or corporation]

I, declare under penalty of perjury that I have read the answers contained in the foregoing statement of financial affairs and any attachments thereto and that they are true and correct to the best of my knowledge, information and belief.

Date _____   Signature _____

                                _____
                                Print Name and Title

[An individual signing on behalf of a partnership or corporation must indicate position or relationship to debtor.]

_____ continuation sheets attached

Penalty for making a false statement: Fine of up to $500,000 or imprisonment for up to 5 years, or both. 18 U.S.C. § 152 and 3571

Statement of Financial Affairs, continued

Form B8
6/90

Form 8. CHAPTER 7 INDIVIDUAL DEBTOR'S STATEMENT OF INTENTION

[Caption as in Form 16B]

CHAPTER 7 INDIVIDUAL DEBTOR'S STATEMENT OF INTENTION

1. I, the debtor, have filed a schedule of assets and liabilities which includes consumer debts secured by property of the estate.

2. My intention with respect to the property of the estate which secures those consumer debts is as follows:

    a. *Property to Be Surrendered.*

Description of Property	Creditor's name
1. _____	_____
2. _____	_____
3. _____	_____

    b. *Property to Be Retained. [Check applicable statement of debtor's intention concerning reaffirmation, redemption, or lien avoidance.]*

Description of property	Creditor's name	Debt will be reaffirmed pursuant to § 524(c)	Property is claimed as exempt and will be redeemed pursuant to § 722	Lien will be avoided pursuant to § 522(f) and property will be claimed as exempt
1. _____	_____	_____	_____	_____
2. _____	_____	_____	_____	_____
3. _____	_____	_____	_____	_____
4. _____	_____	_____	_____	_____
5. _____	_____	_____	_____	_____

3. I understand that § 521(2)(B) of the Bankruptcy Code requires that I perform the above stated intention within 45 days of the filing of this statement with the court, or within such additional time as the court, for cause, within such 45-day period fixes.

Date: _____

                         _____
                         Signature of Debtor

Individual Debtor's Statement of Intention

FORM B9A
6/90

United States Bankruptcy Court

Case Number

_____ District of _____

NOTICE OF COMMENCEMENT OF CASE UNDER CHAPTER 7 OF THE BANKRUPTCY CODE,
MEETING OF CREDITORS, AND FIXING OF DATES
(Individual or Joint Debtor No Asset Case)

In re (Name of Debtor)	Address of Debtor	Soc. Sec./Tax Id. Nos.
	Date Case Filed (or Converted)	
Name and Address of Attorney for Debtor	Name and Address of Trustee	
Telephone Number		Telephone Number

☐ This is a converted case originally filed under chapter _____ on _____ (date).

DATE, TIME, AND LOCATION OF MEETING OF CREDITORS

DISCHARGE OF DEBTS

Deadline to File a Complaint Objecting to Discharge of the Debtor or to Determine Dischargeability of Certain Types of Debts:

AT THIS TIME THERE APPEAR TO BE NO ASSETS AVAILABLE FROM WHICH PAYMENT MAY BE MADE TO UNSECURED CREDITORS. DO NOT FILE A PROOF OF CLAIM UNTIL YOU RECEIVE NOTICE TO DO SO.

COMMENCEMENT OF CASE. A petition for liquidation under chapter 7 of the Bankruptcy Code has been filed in this court by or against the person or persons named above as the debtor, and an order for relief has been entered. You will not receive notice of all documents filed in this case. All documents filed with the court, including lists of the debtor's property, debts, and property claimed as exempt are available for inspection at the office of the clerk of the bankruptcy court.

CREDITORS MAY NOT TAKE CERTAIN ACTIONS. A creditor is anyone to whom the debtor owes money or property. Under the Bankruptcy Code, the debtor is granted certain protection against creditors. Common examples of prohibited actions by creditors are contacting the debtor to demand repayment, taking action against the debtor to collect money owed to creditors or to take property of the debtor, and starting or continuing foreclosure actions, repossessions, or wage deductions. If unauthorized actions are taken by a creditor against a debtor, the court may penalize that creditor. A creditor who is considering taking action against the debtor or the property of the debtor should review § 362 of the Bankruptcy Code and may wish to seek legal advice. The staff of the clerk of the bankruptcy court is not permitted to give legal advice.

MEETING OF CREDITORS. The debtor (both husband and wife in a joint case) is required to appear at the meeting of creditors on the date and at the place set forth above for the purpose of being examined under oath. Attendance by creditors at the meeting is welcomed, but not required. At the meeting, the creditors may elect a trustee other than the one named above, elect a committee of creditors, examine the debtor, and transact such other business as may properly come before the meeting. The meeting may be continued or adjourned from time to time by notice at the meeting, without further written notice to creditors.

LIQUIDATION OF THE DEBTOR'S PROPERTY. The trustee will collect the debtor's property and turn any that is not exempt into money. At this time, however, it appears from the schedules of the debtor that there are no assets from which any distribution can be paid to creditors. If at a later date it appears that there are assets from which a distribution may be paid, the creditors will be notified and given an opportunity to file claims.

EXEMPT PROPERTY. Under state and federal law, the debtor is permitted to keep certain money or property as exempt. If a creditor believes that an exemption of money or property is not authorized by law, the creditor may file an objection. An objection must be filed not later than 30 days after the conclusion of the meeting of creditors.

DISCHARGE OF DEBTS. The debtor is seeking a discharge of debts. A discharge means that certain debts are made unenforceable against the debtor personally. Creditors whose claims against the debtor are discharged may never take action against the debtor to collect the discharged debts. If a creditor believes that the debtor should not receive any discharge of debts under § 727 of the Bankruptcy Code or that a debt owed to the creditor is not dischargeable under § 523(a)(2), (4), or (6) of the Bankruptcy Code, timely action must be taken in the bankruptcy court by the deadline set forth above in the box labeled "Discharge of Debts." Creditors considering taking such action may wish to seek legal advice.

DO NOT FILE A PROOF OF CLAIM UNLESS YOU RECEIVE A COURT NOTICE TO DO SO

Address of the Clerk of the Bankruptcy Court	For the Court:
	Clerk of the Bankruptcy Court
	Date

**Notice of Commencement of Case Under Chapter 7 of the Bankruptcy Code,
Meeting of Creditors, and Fixing of Dates: No Asset Case**

FORM B9C
6/90

United States Bankruptcy Court

Case Number

——————— District of ———————

NOTICE OF COMMENCEMENT OF CASE UNDER CHAPTER 7 OF THE BANKRUPTCY CODE, MEETING OF CREDITORS, AND FIXING OF DATES
(Individual or Joint Debtor Asset Case)

In re (Name of Debtor)	Address of Debtor	Soc. Sec./Tax Id. Nos.
	Date Case Filed (or Converted)	

Name and Address of Attorney for Debtor		Name and Address of Trustee	
	Telephone Number		Telephone Number

☐ This is a converted case originally filed under chapter _____ on _____ (date).

FILING CLAIMS

Deadline to file a proof of claim:

DATE, TIME, AND LOCATION OF MEETING OF CREDITORS

DISCHARGE OF DEBTS

Deadline to File a Complaint Objecting to Discharge of the Debtor or to Determine Dischargeability of Certain Types of Debts:

COMMENCEMENT OF CASE. A petition for liquidation under chapter 7 of the Bankruptcy Code has been filed in this court by or against the person or persons named above as the debtor, and an order for relief has been entered. You will not receive notice of all documents filed in this case. All documents filed with the court, including lists of the debtor's property, debts, and property claimed as exempt are available for inspection at the office of the clerk of the bankruptcy court.

CREDITORS MAY NOT TAKE CERTAIN ACTIONS. A creditor is anyone to whom the debtor owes money or property. Under the Bankruptcy Code, the debtor is granted certain protection against creditors. Common examples of prohibited actions by creditors are contacting the debtor to demand repayment, taking action against the debtor to collect money owed to creditors or to take property of the debtor, and starting or continuing foreclosure actions, repossessions, or wage deductions. If unauthorized actions are taken by a creditor against a debtor, the court may penalize that creditor. A creditor who is considering taking action against the debtor or the property of the debtor should review § 362 of the Bankruptcy Code and may wish to seek legal advice. The staff of the clerk of the bankruptcy court is not permitted to give legal advice.

MEETING OF CREDITORS. The debtor (both husband and wife in a joint case) is required to appear at the meeting of creditors on the date and at the place set forth above for the purpose of being examined under oath. Attendance by creditors at the meeting is welcomed, but not required. At the meeting, the creditors may elect a trustee other than the one named above, elect a committee of creditors, examine the debtor, and transact such other business as may properly come before the meeting. The meeting may be continued or adjourned from time to time by notice at the meeting, without further written notice to creditors.

LIQUIDATION OF THE DEBTOR'S PROPERTY. The trustee will collect the debtor's property and turn any that is not exempt into money. If the trustee can collect enough money and property from the debtor, creditors may be paid some or all of the debts owed to them.

EXEMPT PROPERTY. Under state and federal law, the debtor is permitted to keep certain money or property as exempt. If a creditor believes that an exemption of money or property is not authorized by law, the creditor may file an objection. An objection must be filed not later than 30 days after the conclusion of the meeting of creditors.

DISCHARGE OF DEBTS. The debtor is seeking a discharge of debts. A discharge means that certain debts are made unenforceable against the debtor personally. Creditors whose claims against the debtor are discharged may never take action against the debtor to collect the discharged debts. If a creditor believes that the debtor should not receive any discharge of debts under § 727 of the Bankruptcy Code or that a debt owed to the creditor is not dischargeable under § 523(a)(2), (4), or (6) of the Bankruptcy Code, timely action must be taken in the bankruptcy court by the deadline set forth above in the box labeled "Discharge of Debts." Creditors considering taking such action may wish to seek legal advice.

PROOF OF CLAIM. Except as otherwise provided by law, in order to share in any payment from the estate, a creditor must file a proof of claim by the date set forth above in the box labeled "Filing Claims." The place to file the proof of claim, either in person or by mail, is the office of the clerk of the bankruptcy court. Proof of claim forms are available in the clerk's office of any bankruptcy court.

Address of the Clerk of the Bankruptcy Court	For the Court:
	Clerk of the Bankruptcy Court
	Date

Notice of Commencement of Case Under Chapter 7 of the Bankruptcy Code, Meeting of Creditors, and Fixing of Dates: Asset Case

FORM B9I 6/90	**United States Bankruptcy Court**	Case Number

———————————— District of ————————————

**NOTICE OF COMMENCEMENT OF CASE UNDER CHAPTER 13 OF THE BANKRUPTCY CODE,
MEETING OF CREDITORS, AND FIXING OF DATES**

In re (Name of Debtor)	Address of Debtor	Soc. Sec./Tax Id. Nos.
	Date Case Filed (or Converted)	
Name and Address of Attorney for Debtor	Name and Address of Trustee	
Telephone Number	Telephone Number	

☐ This is a converted case originally filed under chapter ——— on ——————————— (date).

FILING CLAIMS

Deadline to file a proof of claim:

DATE, TIME, AND LOCATION OF MEETING OF CREDITORS

FILING OF PLAN AND DATE, TIME, AND LOCATION OF HEARING ON CONFIRMATION OF PLAN

☐ The debtor has filed a plan. The plan or a summary of the plan is enclosed. Hearing on confirmation will be held:

——————————— (Date) ——————————— (Time) ——————————————— (Location)

☐ The debtor has filed a plan. The plan or a summary of the plan and notice of the confirmation hearing will be sent separately.

☐ The debtor has not filed a plan as of this date. Creditors will be given separate notice of the hearing on confirmation of the plan.

COMMENCEMENT OF CASE. An individual's debt adjustment case under chapter 13 of the Bankruptcy Code has been filed in this court by the debtor or debtors named above, and an order for relief has been entered. You will not receive notice of all documents filed in this case. All documents filed with the court, including lists of the debtor's property and debts, are available for inspection at the office of the clerk of the bankruptcy court.

CREDITORS MAY NOT TAKE CERTAIN ACTIONS. A creditor is anyone to whom the debtor owes money. Under the Bankruptcy Code, the debtor is granted certain protection against creditors. Common examples of prohibited actions by creditors are contacting the debtor to demand repayment, taking action against the debtor to collect money owed to creditors or to take property of the debtor, and starting or continuing foreclosure actions, repossessions, or wage deductions. Some protection is also given to certain codebtors of consumer debts. If unauthorized actions are taken by a creditor against a debtor, or a protected codebtor, the court may punish that creditor. A creditor who is considering taking action against the debtor or the property of the debtor, or any codebtor, should review §§ 362 and 1301 of the Bankruptcy Code and may wish to seek legal advice. The staff of the clerk of the bankruptcy court is not permitted to give legal advice.

MEETING OF CREDITORS. The debtor (both husband and wife in a joint case) is required to appear at the meeting of creditors on the date and at the place set forth above in the box labeled "Date, Time, and Location of Meeting of Creditors" for the purpose of being examined under oath. Attendance by creditors at the meeting is welcome, but not required. At the meeting, the creditors may examine the debtor and transact such other business as may properly come before the meeting. The meeting may be continued or adjourned from time to time by notice at the meeting, without further written notice to creditors.

PROOF OF CLAIM. Except as otherwise provided by law, in order to share in any payment from the estate, a creditor must file a proof of claim by the date set forth above in the box labeled "Filing Claims." The place to file the proof of claim, either in person or by mail, is the office of the clerk of the bankruptcy court. Proof of claim forms are available in the clerk's office of any bankruptcy court.

PURPOSE OF A CHAPTER 13 FILING. Chapter 13 of the Bankruptcy Code is designed to enable a debtor to pay debts in full or in part over a period of time pursuant to a plan. A plan is not effective unless approved by the bankruptcy court at a confirmation hearing. Creditors will be given notice in the event the case is dismissed or converted to another chapter of the Bankruptcy Code.

Address of the Clerk of the Bankruptcy Court	For the Court:
	Clerk of the Bankruptcy Court
	Date

**Notice of Commencement of Case Under Chapter 13 of the Bankruptcy Code,
Meeting of Creditors, and Fixing of Dates**

Form B16A
6/90

Form 16A. CAPTION (FULL)

UNITED STATES BANKRUPTCY COURT
_____DISTRICT OF_____

In re _____,)
      [Set forth here all names including married,)
      maiden, and trade names used by debtor within)
      last 6 years.])
                                        Debtor)   Case No. _____
)
)   Chapter _____
)
Social Security No(s). _____ and all)
Employer's Tax Identification Nos. *[if any]* _____)
                     _____)

[Designation of Character of Paper]

Caption: Long Form

Form B16B
6/90

Form 16B. CAPTION (SHORT TITLE)

UNITED STATES BANKRUPTCY COURT
_____ DISTRICT OF _____

In re _____,
                       Debtor

Case No. _____

Chapter _____

[Designation of Character of Paper]

Caption: Short Form

Form B18
6/90

Form 18. DISCHARGE OF DEBTOR

[Caption as in Form 16A]

DISCHARGE OF DEBTOR

It appearing that a petition commencing a case under title 11, United States Code, was filed by or against the person named above on _____, and that an order for relief was entered under chapter 7, and that no complaint objecting to the discharge of the debtor was filed within the time fixed by the court [*or* that a complaint objecting to discharge of the debtor was filed and, after due notice and hearing, was not sustained];

IT IS ORDERED that

1. The above-named debtor is released from all dischargeable debts.

2. Any judgment heretofore or hereafter obtained in any court other than this court is null and void as a determination of the personal liability of the debtor with respect to any of the following:

(a) debts dischargeable under 11 U.S.C. § 523;

(b) unless heretofore or hereafter determined by order of this court to be nondischargeable, debts alleged to be excepted from discharge under clauses (2), (4) and (6) of 11 U.S.C. § 523(a);

(c) debts determined by this court to be discharged.

3. All creditors whose debts are discharged by this order and all creditors whose judgments are declared null and void by paragraph 2 above are enjoined from instituting or continuing any action or employing any process or engaging in any act to collect such debts as personal liabilities of the above-named debtor.

Dated: _____

BY THE COURT

_____
United States Bankruptcy Judge.

Discharge of Debtor

Appendix B:

In re Bachmann

UNITED STATES BANKRUPTCY COURT
FOR THE SOUTHERN DISTRICT
OF FLORIDA

```
                                    )
                                    )
In re:                              )
                                    )
CHRISTOPHER BACHMANN,               )  CASE NO. 88-04588-BKC-AJC
CHARLENE RAE BACHMANN,              )
                                    )  CHAPTER 13 CASE
           Debtors                  )
                                    )
_____)
```

ᴕ

MEMORANDUM OPINION

On November 15, 1988, the debtors, Christopher
Bachmann and Charlene Rae Bachmann, filed a joint bankruptcy
petition under Chapter 13 of the United States Bankruptcy Code.
During the administration of this case, it was alleged that a
typing service in South Florida was abusing the Bankruptcy
system.

At the confirmation hearing on December 20, 1988, the
Chapter 13 trustee advised the Court that he had examined the
Chapter 13 plan and discussed the plan with the debtors at the
first meeting of creditors. The trustee advised the debtors
that the plan was improperly prepared and could not be
recommended for confirmation. The Chapter 13 plan as filed by
the debtors was vague, indefinite, contrary to the Code, and
only provided for payment of twenty percent of the unsecured
indebtedness, notwithstanding available additional income.

The debtors told the Chapter 13 trustee that the debtors knew nothing about Chapter 13 nor did they understand how to prepare or file a plan. The debtors told the trustee that a typing service advised them to file a Chapter 13 petition and prepared the plan for them. The debtors identified Paul C. Meyer of Capital Business Services, Inc. as the typing service.

The Court, sua sponte, entered an "Order to Show Cause Why Paul C. Meyer and Capital Business Services, Inc. Should Not Be Held in Contempt of Court For The Unauthorized Practice of Law" and set a hearing thereon. The hearing was convened twice and continued twice at the request of Mr. Meyer. Thereafter, the United States Trustee, on the order of this court, began an investigation, and, on March 17, 1989, filed a Motion For En Banc Hearing To Find Paul C. Meyer of Capital Business Services, Inc. In Civil Contempt Of Court and Other Relief (C. P. No. 25a).

An Evidentiary Hearing was held on March 31, 1989. Paul C. Meyer and Capital Business Services, Inc. were represented by David C. Vladeck and Allan B. Morrison of Public Citizen Litigation Group. The Assistant United States Trustee appeared by counsel.

There is little factual dispute. Paul C. Meyer was forthright and candid. He testified that he is the vice president of Capital Business Services, Inc. (hereinafter referred to as Capital). It is not disputed that he is not a

2

licensed attorney-at-law.   Mr. Meyer testified that Capital provides services similar to those provided the debtors in this case to individuals who desire to file voluntary petitions for bankruptcy.   Capital also sells bankruptcy forms to debtors. Mr. Meyer described the services performed.   Based on his testimony and the documentary evidence, it appears that Mr. Meyer d/b/a Capital did more than merely sell and type the bankruptcy forms.   The evidence indicates that Mr. Meyer d/b/a Capital, is or has been engaging in the unauthorized practice of law.

Capital advertised in The Flyer and The Pennysaver, local community newspapers.   The advertisements suggest that Capital provides bankruptcy services.   See Appendix, Exhibits A, B, C, D.   The Bachmanns, suffering financial misfortune, read one of these advertisements.   On October 5, 1988, the Bachmanns went to Capital.   At Capital, the Bachmanns were given Mr. Meyer's business card which indicates that Mr. Meyers is a trained paralegal.   See Appendix, Exhibit E.   The Court is unaware of any authority allowing a paralegal to practice law, assist in the practice of law, or provide services to clients where the paralegal is not supervised by a licensed attorney at law.

Mr. Meyer d/b/a Capital held himself out, through both newspaper advertisements and his business card, as being qualified to provide legal services as a paralegal to individual debtors who are in need of the relief provided under

3

the Bankruptcy Code. According to Mr. Bachmann's testimony, Mr. Meyer not only selected the bankruptcy Chapter for the debtors, but also prepared the plan and prepared the debtors' petition.

Mr. Meyer prepared a "Notice to Individual Consumer Debtor(s)." The "Notice To Individual Consumer Debtor(s)", signed by both debtors and dated November 2, 1988 has an "x" typed in front of "chapter 13." This notice does not require an "x" at this point. The document is a certification by the debtors that they have read and presumably understand the options available to them. Apparently, neither the debtors nor Mr. Meyer understand this form or know how to complete it.

The court file contains the Voluntary Joint Petition, neatly typed. The remainder of the schedules are also neatly typed. The Chapter 13 plan, under Section 2(c), consists of only the following typed paragraph:

> Payments for and towards the UNSECURED DEBTS of $15,298.26 shall be made to the extent of only 20% of the indebtedness to each creditor, and without interest, in no more than 12 payments and should such 20% of proved and allowed unsecured indebtedness be sooner paid out before the designated 12 month period, the payments and debt obligations of the debtor shall terminate thereat.

This language does not state a confirmable plan. The debtors told the trustee that they neither composed nor understood this language. This language is not the product of the debtors. It is the language of Mr. Meyer, and it is insufficient.

4

A good definition of what constitutes the practice of law is set forth in <u>Howton v. Morrow</u>, 106 S.W.2d 81 (Ky. Ct. App. 1937) which says:

> The practice of law is not limited to the conduct of cases in Court. According to generally understood definition of the practice of law in this country, it embraces the preparation of pleadings and other papers incident to actions and special proceedings and the management of such actions and proceedings on behalf of clients before Judges and Courts and, in addition, conveyancing, the preparation of legal instruments of all kinds and, in general, all advice to clients and all action taken for them in matters connected with the law and, 'attorney at law' is one who engages in any of these branches of the practice of law. <u>Id</u>. at 83.

In the opinions that the Court has reviewed with regard to the unauthorized practice of law before United States Bankruptcy Courts, the courts have looked to state law for guidance.[1]   <u>In re Anderson</u>, 79 B.R. 482 (Bankr. S.D. Cal. 1987); <u>In re Arthur</u>, 15 B.R. 541 (Bankr. E.D. Pa. 1981); <u>In re Preston</u>, 82 B.R. 28 (Bankr. W.D. Va. 1987). Accordingly, it is appropriate for this Court to look to Florida law with regard to the instant matter.

Persons not licensed as attorneys-at-law are prohibited from practicing law within the State of Florida.

---

[1] It should be noted that another Division of this Court has dismissed a debtor's petition where the unauthorized practice of law was involved.

Fla. Const. of 1968 art. V. § 15 (1989). The Supreme Court of
Florida broadly defines the practice of law. In State v.
Sperry, 140 So.2d 587, 591 (Fla. 1962) the Supreme Court of
Florida stated that:

> ....if the giving of such advice and
> performance of such services affects
> important rights of a person under the law,
> and if the reasonable protection of the
> rights and property of those advised and
> served requires that the persons giving
> such advice possess legal skill and a
> knowledge of the law greater than that
> possessed by the average citizen, then the
> giving of such advice and the performance
> of such services by one for another as a
> course of conduct constitutes the practice
> of law.

In determining whether a particular act constitutes
the practice of law, the Court's concern is the protection of
the public. However, any limitation on the free practice of
law necessarily affects important constitutional rights. This
decision definitely affects Mr. Meyer's constitutional right
to pursue a lawful business. This decision also affects Mr.
Meyer's First Amendment right to speak and print what he
chooses. However, the Court must balance Mr. Meyer's rights
against the public policy of protecting the public from being
advised and represented in legal matters by unqualified persons
over whom the judicial department can exercise little, if any,
control in the matter of infractions of the Code of conduct
which, in the public interest, lawyers are bound to observe.
Sperry, at 595.

6

Florida Bar v. Brumbaugh, 355 So.2d 1186 (Fla. 1978), clearly stated which services secretarial businesses in the State of Florida may lawfully provide. The Supreme Court of Florida held that secretarial services may sell printed materials purporting to explain legal practice and procedure to the public in general and may sell sample legal forms. Id. at 1194. The Supreme Court further held that such businesses may provide secretarial services and type forms for clients, provided that this involves only copying the information given in writing by clients. Id. Additionally, the Florida Supreme Court allowed secretarial services to advertise their business of providing secretarial, notary and typing services, as well as providing legal forms and printed general information. The Supreme Court held that secretarial services may not engage in advising clients as to the various remedies available to the clients, or to otherwise assist them in preparing forms... (emphasis added). Id. The Supreme Court held that secretarial services may not make inquiries nor answer questions from their clients as to, (1) the particular forms which might be necessary, (2) how to best fill out such forms, and (3) how to present necessary evidence at court hearings. Id.

The Brumbaugh opinion has been consistently followed by the Supreme Court of Florida in The Florida Bar v. Furman, 376 So.2d 378 (Fla. 1979); The Florida Bar v. Furman, 451 So.2d 808 (Fla. 1984); The Florida Bar v. Weissman, 508 So.2d 327 (Fla. 1987).

7

In <u>Brumbaugh</u>, the Florida Supreme Court's opinion
dealt with the unlicensed practice of law in the context of
dissolution of marriages. Nonetheless, it applies to other
unauthorized legal assistance. The Florida Supreme Court
indicated in its ruling that <u>Brumbaugh</u> would apply to other
activities. <u>Id</u>. The Supreme Court cited the preparation of
wills and real estate transactions as examples of such
activities. <u>Id</u>. Secretarial services may sell legal forms for
appropriate proceedings, and type instruments with data or
information supplied by their clients. However, secretarial
services may not engage in personal legal assistance in
conjunction with business activities. This Court believes that
the Supreme Court of Florida did not intend a limited
application of its opinion. Accordingly, the Court holds that
the opinion in <u>Brumbaugh</u> is correctly applied to the instant
case.

   The Court finds that Mr. Meyer d/b/a Capital was
engaged in the unauthorized practice of law. The advice and
counselling which Mr. Meyer d/b/a Capital provided the debtor
concerning Bankruptcy law constitutes the unauthorized practice
of law. The advice and counselling given to the debtors in
this case constitutes the unauthorized practice of law because
such advice requires the use of legal judgment requiring legal
knowledge, training, skill, and ability beyond that possessed
by the average lay person. The drafting and preparation of
various legal documents by Mr. Meyer, including Chapter 13

8

petitions, statements, and schedules, on a regular basis for a fee constitutes the unauthorized practice of law. The act of soliciting debtors constitutes the solicitation for the unauthorized practice of law because these advertisements imply that Mr. Meyer d/b/a/ Capital is qualified to perform legal services. Mr. Meyer also engaged in the unauthorized practice of law when he solicited information from the Bachmanns which he reformulated and typed into their bankruptcy petition. Further, Mr. Meyer and/or Capital conducted the unauthorized practice of law when he advised the debtors to file a Chapter 13 Petition and when he composed the debtors' insufficient Chapter 13 plan.

Although Mr. Meyer d/b/a Capital Business Services, Inc. has engaged in the unauthorized practice of law in this case, the Court is satisfied that Mr. Meyer's actions were without intent to violate the law. Therefore, the Court does not determine Mr. Meyer to be in contempt of this Court. Rather it is deemed appropriate to enjoin Mr. Meyer d/b/a Capital Business Services, Inc. from further engaging in the unauthorized practice of law.

In order to assist Mr. Meyer d/b/a Capital and other typing services in determining what services may and may not be provided to possible debtors, the Court offers the following guidelines.

"Typing services", including Mr. Meyer, may type bankruptcy forms for their clients, provided they only copy the written information furnished by his clients. They may not advise clients as to the various remedies and procedures available in the Bankruptcy system. Mr. Meyer and representatives of typing services may not make inquiries nor answer questions as to the completion of particular bankruptcy forms or schedules nor advise how to best fill out bankruptcy forms or complete schedules. They may legally sell bankruptcy forms and any printed material purporting to explain bankruptcy practice and procedure to the public. Under no circumstance may they engage in personal legal assistance in conjunction with typing service business activities, including the correction of errors and omissions.

A problem arises when information is taken orally. Under these circumstances, we are faced with determining what was actually said. From Mr. Meyer's testimony, it is clear that his memory is not good in that area and the memory or notes of a typing service representative are not sufficient. There were numerous questions asked about what was said that Mr. Meyer just did not remember. Accordingly, it is suggested that typing services may take information from clients orally provided that they record the conversations and preserve the tapes. These tapes must be available at the first meeting of creditors. There is no reason why Mr. Meyer or others cannot charge additional compensation for the cost of using and storing the tapes. The small charge will be more than offset by the precision of the record.

10

Another problem arises with regard to advertising. Mr. Meyer is enjoined from using the word "paralegal" on his business cards. Mr. Meyers may advertise his business activities of providing secretarial, notary, and/or typing services. Mr. Meyer may also advertise that he sells bankruptcy forms and general printed information with regard to those forms. However, Mr. Meyer may not advertise in any misleading fashion which leads a reasonable lay person to believe that he offers the public legal services, legal advice or legal assistance regarding Bankruptcy.

Neither Mr. Meyer, nor his company, claim to be an attorney at law. 11 U.S.C. § 329 covers debtors and transactions with attorneys, including attorneys who are not attorneys-at-law. It states in part:

> Any attorney representing a debtor in a case under this title, or in connection with such a case,....

Congress did not define "attorney" in Section 101 of the Code, and therefore, it is appropriate to use a broad definition for attorney. "An attorney is one who is legally appointed by another to transact business for him." Webster's New Collegiate Dictionary 72 (7th ed. 1965). Examples of attorneys that are not attorneys-at-law are attorneys-in-fact and powers of attorney.

Clearly, Mr. Meyer and his company meet that definition. If he is in the form-preparing business and someone comes to his business establishment and requests legal

11

forms be typed for a charge, that is a lawful attorney (not an attorney-at-law) relationship under the Webster Dictionary definition. The Court believes that this definition is broad enough to fit within the area to which Congress referred when enacting Section 329, Title 11, U.S. Code.

Section 329 deals with the compensation paid by debtors. It has two purposes. The first purpose is to protect debtors from paying exorbitant or unreasonable compensation which would be to their own detriment and to the detriment of the unsecured creditors of an estate. Section 329 also prevents dishonest debtors from making disparate payments to unentitled persons so that the bankruptcy estate would be diminished to the detriment of unsecured creditors. For this reason Congress provided under Section 329 that such compensation is subject to review.

Additionally, Bankruptcy Rule 2017 provides that:

> On motion by any party in interest or on the court's own initiative, the court after notice and a hearing may determine whether any payment of money or any transfer of property by the debtor, made directly or indirectly and in contemplation of the filing of a petition under the Code by or against the debtor, to an attorney for services rendered or to be rendered is excessive.

In this case the United States Trustee in its Motion and report moved to review the compensation. It is appropriate to review the compensation of Mr. Meyer d/b/a Capital and to determine whether or not the compensation was appropriate for the services rendered. 11 U.S. C. § 329 (1984).

12

Mr. Meyer testified that it takes approximately one and a half hours to two hours to type the bankruptcy forms. The bankruptcy forms required to file a petition cost approximately ten dollars ($10.00). Allowing for a reasonable typing fee as well as a reasonable profit on the bankruptcy forms sold to the debtors, the Court finds that under all the circumstances of the instant case a reasonable fee is $60.00 for the selling of the bankruptcy forms to the debtors and typing the relevant information. Accordingly, it is

ORDERED that Mr. Meyer return to the Chapter 13 trustee in this case, the sum of $50.00. This sum represents the difference between the $110.00 fee which the debtors were charged by Mr. Meyer d/b/a Capital for the preparation of their Chapter 13 Petition and the $60.00 determined to be a reasonable fee in this case.

The Court in its ruling is sympathetic to the needs of indigent debtors. The Court must also be cognizant of the purpose for which Congress enacted the Bankruptcy Code. This decision is not made to protect the members of the legal profession either in creating or maintaining a monopoly or closed shop. Tragically there are few attorneys-at-law available to represent debtors in this fee range. This opinion is entered specifically to clarify congressional efforts to protect the public from being advised and represented in bankruptcy legal matters by unqualified persons and to protect them from being overcharged. Further, the Court must take into account the rights of the innocent creditors which may be adversely impacted. Therefore, after consideration, it is

ORDERED as follows:

1. Paul C. Meyer, d/b/a Capital Business Services, Inc., is permanently enjoined and restrained from engaging in the unauthorized practice of law.

2. Paul C. Meyer d/b/a Capital Business Services, Inc., is enjoined from advertising such as that set forth in Exhibits A, B, C, and D attached hereto.

3. Paul C. Meyer d/b/a Capital Business Services, Inc., is enjoined from using the title paralegal or advertising himself as a paralegal. He may seek dissolution of this portion of the injunction upon presentation of adequate evidence that he is qualified to be a paralegal and is working under the supervision of a licensed attorney.

4. Paul C. Meyer d/b/a Capital Business Services, Inc., is directed to turn over to the trustee herein the sum of $50 as a return of excessive compensation, pursuant to 11 U.S.C. § 329.

DONE and ORDERED at Miami, Florida this 30 day of March, 1990.

A. Jay Cristol

A. JAY CRISTOL
Judge. U.S. Bankruptcy Court

14

Appendix C:

In re Davis & Associates, P.C.

UNITED STATES BANKRUPTCY COURT
WESTERN DISTRICT OF TEXAS
SAN ANTONIO DIVISION

IN RE	§	
	§	MISC. CASE NO.
DAVIS & ASSOCIATES, P.C.	§	
	§	92-509
	§	

ORDER UPON HEARING OF ORDER TO APPEAR AND SHOW CAUSE

CAME ON for hearing and consideration upon this court's order to appear and show cause the law firm of Davis & Associates, P.C. The court has determined that cause has not been shown. The firm has engaged in conduct which this court finds renders it necessary (1) to permanently bar said firm from further practice in the bankruptcy courts for the Western District of Texas, (2) to prohibit said firm from further representing clients in said courts, and (3) to re-assign all of its bankruptcy cases to other lawyers.

The court finds the following, in support of its ruling:

1. The law firm engaged in extensive advertising in the San Antonio area, including expensive, highly effective television advertising, representing to consumers of bankruptcy services in the community that the firm was skilled and effective at handling bankruptcy matters.[1] In fact, the firm was only formed in April of 1992. Its bankruptcy "department" was

---

[1] For months, the firm ran well-done spots in the 7:30 a.m. - 8:00 a.m. slot during the morning national news programs (*Today, Good Morning America, This Morning*). The ads gave the impression that the firm was a well-established firm of skilled bankruptcy specialists competent to handle consumer bankruptcy matters. Nothing in the ad revealed that the firm was newly formed or that its bankruptcy lawyer was a novice. The service area of the local television stations includes towns located in the Southern District of Texas, and some of the bankruptcy filings of the firm were in the Corpus Christi and Victoria Divisions of the Southern District of Texas.

staffed only by Frank Edward Taylor, a two year lawyer with no prior bankruptcy experience operating with no supervision, together with various paralegals. At the time he commenced his bankruptcy practice with Davis & Associates (and at the time the media campaign was commenced), he was not even licensed to practice in federal court.[2] The lawyer was not capable of rendering competent bankruptcy services to consumer debtors, especially not on a volume basis, without guidance or supervision, nor should he have been offering legal services in this area without appropriate legal training in consumer bankruptcy.

2. One of the firm's principle architects was Larry Majors, a non-lawyer who helped design the firm's advertising and apparently crafted some of the firm's practices, such as routinely demanding post-dated checks as a pre-condition to handling a debtor's bankruptcy case (especially in chapter 7 cases), conducting initial interviews using nonlawyer staff, and paying a sign-up bonus to paralegals. Mr. Majors represented himself as an expert at administering a law office, someone who could make a firm so valuable that he was worth paying a lot. And he *was* paid a lot. While the attorney handling the bankruptcy cases was paid $20,000 a year (increased later to $24,000), and Marvin Davis, the firm's principle

---

[2] Indeed, he did not obtain his license until the court refused to grant further applications for admission *pro hac vice*. The court wrote the attorney in July that it was disturbed that the firm was promoting its bankruptcy expertise so heavily in the media yet its only bankruptcy attorney was not even licensed to practice in the bankruptcy courts of this district. The court in its correspondence even then described the practice as "deceptive."

was paid approximately $36,000 a year, Mr. Majors was paid $8,000 a month (an annual salary of $96,000). The firm also paid for his car (a Bentley) and perhaps for his housing as well.

3. Intake interviews were routinely conducted by non-lawyers, with whom the decision whether to file bankruptcy was made, as well as the decision whether to file under chapter 7 or chapter 13. Both Larry Majors and his son Austin Majors heavily participated in this process. Some debtors reported that they were led to believe that Larry Majors was an attorney. A few were told in so many words that Larry Majors was an attorney. Promises and representations were made to clients by these paralegals regarding the benefits of bankruptcy, and many clients were given misinformation regarding what bankruptcy could do for them. Routinely, paralegals were paid a $20 bonus for each new case they signed up. In dozens of documented cases, bankruptcy was filed, the schedules were prepared, and a chapter 13 plan was assembled and filed, all without the clients' ever having met with an attorney. In these cases, the first time the client ever met the attorney was at the first meeting of creditors (not prior to -- *at*). In a number of cases, clients were even asked to sign schedules and statements of affairs in blank, for the paralegals to fill in later.

4. The firm routinely demanded clients pay fees with post-dated checks in both chapter 13 and chapter 7 cases, ostensibly to make it easier for the

3

debtors to pay on "terms." The scheme also allowed the firm to charge far more for representing debtors in chapter 7 then was routinely charged by most attorneys in the San Antonio area.[3] The checks were then cashed, post-filing, with the result that fees incurred pre-petition were being paid post-petition, even though all prepetition obligations (including these fees) were discharged. In some cases, clients were simply sending in checks on a post-petition basis to pay for pre-petition bankruptcy services, even though the Bankruptcy Code does not permit this.[4] This method of payment was never disclosed by the firm in the Disclosure of Compensation which the firm was obligated to file in every bankruptcy case, though it should have been. *See* 11 U.S.C. § 329; FED.R.BANKR.P. 2016(b).[5]

---

[3] Most routine chapter 7 cases in San Antonio are handled for between $500 and $800 a case. *See* discussion *infra.*

[4] In chapter 13 cases, debtor's counsel can only be paid to the extent the fees are approved by the court. 11 U.S.C. § 329, 331. In chapter 7 cases, the services are obtained pre-petition, and the obligation must similarly be paid for before the case is filed. Otherwise, the bill for legal services is discharged, just like any other pre-petition obligation, and the attorney is barred from collecting the bill, just like any other pre-petition creditor, unless the debtor affirmatively re-affirms the debt. *See* 11 U.S.C. § 524(a), (d). The records do not reflect such reaffirmations. Of course, any debtor is free to repay any prepetition debt they choose voluntarily, but debtors were told in these cases that they *had* to repay this debt over time in this fashion in order to file bankruptcy. The firm thus used its position as the debtors' attorney to collect on the obligation owed, without also advising the debtors that the obligation to the firm was discharged by the debtors' bankruptcy. This, of course, was not proper. It was also improper for the firm not to disclose this method of payment in its Disclosure of Compensation filed in each case.

[5] Because of the structure of the firm, the prohibition against the "sharing of compensation" with any entity other than the attorney for the debtor may have been violated. The gross disparity in compensation between Mr. Davis and Mr. Majors, coupled with Mr. Majors' belief that he was entitled to the firm's receivables as a matter of contract, suggests that Davis and Majors had an illegal agreement to share compensation. This fact of course was never disclosed.

4

5.   In virtually every case, clients were charged $1,500, even for routine chapter 7 cases. Yet schedules were not properly filled out in some cases, creditors were often left off, and some clients were given misinformation regarding the effect of their discharge. Chapter 13 plans were routinely incomplete, incorrectly computed, internally inconsistent, or inadequate to deal with the client's problem. Even after repeated prodding from the chapter 13 trustee and the court, the firm seemed incapable of correcting mistakes in these plans.

6.   Judge Ronald B. King, after conducting a hearing on one of the firm's chapter 7 cases (on request of the panel trustee in that case for disgorgement), ordered Mr. Taylor's firm to refund all but $400 of the fee charged, remarking that the fee of $1,500 in a routine chapter 7 case was *prima facie* unreasonable. Meanwhile, this court, in a series of chapter 13 confirmation hearings, reduced and on occasion completely disallowed fees charged by the firm in chapter 13 cases.

7.   The firm was not capable of adequately responding to the needs of its clients. In one case, *In re Carolina Ruiz*, the firm failed to file a bankruptcy case in time to prevent the sale of the debtor's vehicles, even though it knew the deadline by which the case had to be filed. It reassured the debtor that the filing would be made in time, failed to file in time, then failed to advise the debtor of that fact. It then failed to even advise the debtor when she needed to attend the first meeting of

creditors, with the result that her case was dismissed for her failure to appear. The firm took $500 for its services, refused to answer her repeated telephone calls, and refused to refund the money. The case was filed in the Southern District of Texas.

8. The firm had at least 40 files in its office as of the show cause hearing, all cases in which the clients had paid money to have their bankruptcy case filed, but their bankruptcy case had yet to be filed (even though the paralegals in the office had, in many of these cases, sent out letters to creditors advising them that bankruptcy *had been* filed). The monies paid included money for filing fees. Yet the law firm had *never* placed any monies since its inception into the firm's trust account. As of the date of the hearing, at least $6000 should have been in the firm's trust account just to cover the filing fees given to the firm for these 40 files, yet the account had nothing in it.

9. Larry Majors was involved in a similar operation in the Fort Worth, area, called Paternostro & Associates.[7] Similar practices were employed there, and a State Bar of Texas investigation was initiated. Majors convinced Frank Taylor and Marvin Davis (who were also associated with that firm) to come to San Antonio to start this operation here, under the rubric Davis & Associates. Larry Majors fronted the money to set up

---

[6] The number of actual unfiled cases may be higher.

[7] The firm has since been taken over by another firm.

this operation, negotiated a favorable lease, negotiated television commercial time, designed the advertising program, and set up the firm's operations on the same model as that used in the Fort Worth firm. Davis provided the "lawyer" Majors needed to start up his "law firm" operation.

10. Mr. Majors and Mr. Davis (the putative owner of Davis & Associates) had a falling out in October, 1992, at about the same time as some of the practice problems with Davis & Associates were coming to light in the bankruptcy courts. Larry Majors left the firm, taking with him some $300,000 in post-dated checks. About $128,000 of these checks was subsequently negotiated by Mr. Majors, and apparently appropriated to his personal use. These funds of course represented legal fees in bankruptcy cases, some of which were not properly receivable by the firm (because they represented post-petition payment for pre-petition services, and because in many cases they were excessive). As such, these funds were arguably property of the numerous bankruptcy estates to which they were attributable.*

11. Mr. Majors evidently opened up a checking account in the Dallas area, representing that he had signing authority for the firm, then, using a stamp which he either expropriated or fabricated, negotiated checks of

---

* It is not known whether all the checks taken were in fact "post-dated" checks. Some may have been filing fees from various cases taken in by the firm but yet to be filed.

7

Davis & Associates, P.C. As a result of this misappropriation, the firm has suffered losses that render it difficult or impossible for the firm to continue to represent clients in bankruptcy.

12. The firm hired a local attorney, one Phil Yochem, on a contract basis to handle its bankruptcy files, after it could no longer hire attorneys (it was unable to pay the attorney it hired to replace the first bankruptcy attorney, Mr. Frank Taylor). Mr. Frank Taylor left the firm in October 1992, having attracted the attention of the standing chapter 13 trustee and the bankruptcy judges due to his evident inability to adequately represent his clients and handle the responsibilities imposed on lawyers who practice in the bankruptcy courts for this district. Mr. Taylor also had some health problems which made leaving at the time he did propitious. The substitute attorney, Don Emory, was unable to follow through, principally because the firm let him know they could not pay him, within about a month of having hired him.

13. Mr. Yochem attempted to handle the firm's cases, but discovered that the firm had not sent out notices in many cases, even though he had already signed the certificate of service (because it could not afford the postage), that the firm had not filed bankruptcy petitions even though he had assured the clients that the petitions would be filed (because the firm had a backlog and because in some cases, the pre-paid filing fees had disappeared), and that fees ostensibly pre-paid in some cases in fact

8

now could not be accounted for. Upon learning of these difficulties, Mr. Yochem terminated his services.

14. As of the hearing date, the firm was still unable to account for the identity and number of as-yet-unfiled cases in its offices (cases for which it had already been paid some money), was unable to account for trust funds, and had only recovered some, not all, of the post-dated checks from Larry Majors. It finds itself in precarious financial straits, in spite of its affirmative obligations to the many clients it was able to attract with its slick advertising. There are over 450 clients signed up with the firm for bankruptcy cases alone. Apparently, the monies entrusted to the firm for filing fees were spent on operations or misappropriated.

15. In the early days of the firm, a companion organization, South Texas Lawyers Referral Service, owned by Larry Majors' step-father, engaged in heavy television advertising in San Antonio, billing itself as a non-profit, non-affiliated public service organization which would assist in putting persons in touch with a competent law firm to handle their bankruptcy matters. In point of fact, many of the referrals (perhaps as much as 85%) were made solely to Davis & Associates, P.C. In excess of $60,000 in television advertising invoices incurred by this entity were in fact billed to and paid by Davis & Associates, P.C.

The foregoing facts establish that the firm is not competent to handle bankruptcy cases in this (or any) district. In fact, the firm's principle readily agreed on this point, and indicated his desire to get out of this area of practice. Further, the foregoing is a *prima facie* case establishing violations of the Texas Deceptive Trade Practices Act. In addition, the firm has engaged in barratry, and has failed to account for client funds entrusted to it, in flagrant violation of State Bar rules. Finally, the handling of funds, especially Mr. Larry Majors' conduct, may constitute criminal activity.

The evidence presented further indicates that this is not the first time there have been problems with this sort of activity involving these players. Prior to his association with the Fort Worth law firm, Mr. Majors apparently engaged in similar activity in Phoenix, Arizona. His brother Wayne Majors has a similar line of work in Dallas with a firm there. A fair inference to be drawn from the evidence is that Davis & Associates, P.C. was owned by Marvin Davis in name only; that in truth this was Larry Majors' law firm, which he ran for his own benefit and his own profit, with no concern whatsoever for the welfare of the clients, and with no accountability whatsoever to the State Bar of Texas (whom he evidently took to be a toothless tiger). He appears to have enticed persons to come to the firm for legal services the firm was totally incapable of performing, skimmed funds off the top for his personal use (including, perhaps, client trust funds), had the firm pay for advertising bills incurred by his step-father's firm, had the firm pay for his car and perhaps his house, and then misappropriated money and left town, leaving the firm incapable of fulfilling its obligations to its clients. The firm cannot afford to pay a lawyer to handle the files it has in its office, and appears not even to be able to pay its nonlawyer staff.

10

Given the foregoing, it would be irresponsible for this or any federal court to permit such a firm to continue to enjoy the privileges of practice before the federal bankruptcy court. Moreover, the innocent consumers of this community have been victimized by this firm's practices. The integrity of the bankruptcy system has been impugned. Now, as a result of this pattern of conduct, hundreds of people no longer have available to them the legal services for which they paid (and to which they were just entitled), and other members of the bar are going to have to "pick up the pieces," as it were, in all likelihood having to represent these debtors without compensation themselves. This court always has the right to preserve its own integrity, as well as to police the privilege of practice before this court. When the interests of an innocent and unsuspecting public are also at stake, drastic and firm intervention is essential, especially when it appears that they are being victimized by what borders on a criminal enterprise.

For all of the foregoing reasons, it is the order of this court that, effective January 12, 1993, the law firm of Davis & Assoicates, P.C., and its attorneys, are specifically barred from practice before the bankruptcy courts of the Western District of Texas. In view of the imminent danger of misappropriated funds and the total lack of any lawyer currently at the firm even licensed to practice in federal court (much less competent to handle a bankruptcy case), it is no longer feasible for the firm to continue to handle the bankruptcy cases it has. In view of the court's order, the firm is in any event disqualified from appearing in this court.

Accordingly, it is also necessary to officially remove said firm from further representation of any bankruptcy client (including those clients whose cases have not yet been filed), and to re-assign all such cases to other lawyers (subject, of course, to the veto of the clients). The United States Trustee is hereby authorized and directed to assume control over all client files of Davis & Associates, P.C. relating to bankruptcy, and to re-assign all such files, on a blind draw basis, to a panel of attorneys whom the U.S. Trustee may constitute. The U.S. Trustee is further empowered to audit said firm, and said firm and its staff are directed to cooperate with said audit. The audit shall include an accounting for monies paid by clients. The audit shall also include an accounting of the status of all client matters, and documentation relating to the handling of all client matters. The U.S. Trustee is authorized to retain an examiner to assist it in these matters.

The post-dated checks currently held by Davis & Associates, P.C. shall not be negotiated; they shall be turned over to the U.S. Trustee.

Davis & Associates and Marvin Davis shall immediately (by no later than the close of banking business, January 13, 1993) deposit into the firm's trust account the sum of $6,000, to assure that funds are available for filing fees for pending currently unfiled bankruptcy cases. The funds in this account shall be available to the respective clients for filing their bankruptcy cases if they so chose (after their cases have been reassigned to another attorney and they have had an opportunity to discuss whether they desire to file with their new attorney). Davis & Associates and Marvin

12

Davis shall cooperate fully in making these funds available for filing, at the request of the U.S. Trustee.

All funds currently due the law firm for services in pending chapter 13 cases shall not be paid to said firm, but shall be paid to whatever attorneys are assigned the cases. Funds which have already been paid to the firm may be subject to disgorgement upon motion of the chapter 13 trustee and an opportunity for hearing thereon. Such motion may be filed in this miscellaneous case, but shall detail the respective bankruptcy cases in which disgorgement is sought. It shall not be necessary to file disgorgement motion in each separate bankruptcy case.

All debtors in chapter 7 cases who have previously been directed by the firm to make monthly payments to the firm post-petition are hereby relieved of said obligation. The U.S. Trustee is authorized to contact all such debtors and so inform them. Any funds received by said firm from debtors in chapter 7 cases shall be segregated and accounted for to the U.S. Trustee. Funds already received by the firm for chapter 7 services are subject to disgorgement upon motion of the respective chapter 7 panel trustees or upon motion of the U.S. Trustee. Such motion for disgorgement may be filed in this miscellaneous case, but shall make reference to the specific bankruptcy cases in which disgorgement is sought.

All attorneys to whom cases are assigned by the U.S. Trustee have the right to receive payment for such cases to the extent that funds were otherwise to be paid to Davis & Associates. They are expressly released from any liability for any actions of Davis & Associates, and any action against said attorneys for such liability is

13

expressly barred. In confirmed chapter 13 cases, they shall be entitled to receive such funds as are currently designated for payment to Davis & Associates, without having to file a fee application. In unconfirmed chapter 13 cases, they shall be entitled to receive such funds as would otherwise be payable to Davis & Associates as when the plan is confirmed. Attorneys shall not be entitled to further payment except upon application to this court.[9] In chapter 7 cases, debtors who have to date not paid more than $400 for their chapter 7 cases may be required to pay the difference between what they have paid and $400, in order to compensate assigned counsel for such services as may still be necessary in their respective chapter 7 cases.[10]

So ORDERED.

SIGNED this 14th day of January, 1993, *nunc pro tunc as of January 12, 1993.*

———————————————————
LEIF M. CLARK
U. S. Bankruptcy Judge

---

[9] The court is concerned that debtors not have to "pay twice" for the same service, but also recognizes that there may be a few, extraordinary cases in which extra services are required not because of the mistakes of Davis & Associates but because of the exigencies of the client's situation. The court does not anticipate many such situations, nor does the court encourage same.

[10] Assigned substitute counsel would be rendering services by court order *post-petition*, to assure on a quantum meruit basis that counsel is compensated for services for which the debtor had originally contracted anyway. In fairness, debtors ought to receive what they contracted for, but they should also pay for what they expected to receive.

Appendix D:

Selected Secured Credit Card Issuers

American Pacific Bank
P.O. Box 19360
Portland, OR 97280-9360
1-800-879-8745
(Visa; not available to residents of
VT, ME)

Central National Bank
Secured Credit Card Program
Broadway and Charleston at 14th
Mattoon, IL 61938
1-800-876-9119
(Visa and MasterCard)

Community Bank
Spirit Visa Card Program
19590 E. Mainstreet
Parker, CO 80134
303-841-0970 or 1-800-779-8472
(Visa)

Consumer Fresh Start Association
601 Pennsylvania Avenue, N.W.
Suite 900
Washington, DC 20004
1-800-933-CFSA
(Visa; not available to residents of
VT, ME)

First National Bank in Brookings
P.O. Box 6000
Brookings, SD 57006
605-692-2680
(Visa and MasterCard)

First State Bank
P.O. Box 15414
Wilmington, DE 19850
302-322-9111
(Visa and MasterCard)

Key Federal Savings Bank
Secured Card Program
P.O. Box 6057
Havre de Grace, MD 21078-9978
1-800-228-2230 or 410-939-4840
(Visa and MasterCard)

Service One/Bank of Hoven
Secured Visa and MasterCard Program
Service One Card Center
26660 Agoura Road
Calabas, CA 91302
1-800-777-7735
(Visa and MasterCard)

Signet Bank Secured Card
P.O. Box 85547
Richmond, VA 23286-8873
1-800-333-7116
(Visa and MasterCard; not available
to residents of DE, DC, KS, ME, VT,
WI, MO, NM, NC, OR, MA)

Texas Bank, N.A.
1845 Precinct Line Road
Suite 100
Hurst, TX 76054
1-800-451-0273
(Visa)

United Savings Bank
Secured Card Program
711 Van Ness Avenue
San Francisco, CA 94102
1-415-929-6084
(Visa and MasterCard; CA only)

Glossary

adversary proceeding A lawsuit related to a bankruptcy case.

assume You agree to continue performing duties under a contract or lease.

automatic stay An injunction that stops lawsuits, foreclosure, garnishments, and all collection activity. The automatic stay takes effect the moment a bankruptcy petition is filed.

business bankruptcy In a business bankruptcy, the debtor is a business or an individual involved in business, and the debts are for business purposes. Most business bankruptcies are filed under Chapter 11.

Bankruptcy Code The informal name for Title 11 of the United States Code (11 U.S.C. §§ 101 - 1330), the federal law that governs bankruptcies.

Bankruptcy Code exemptions *See exemptions.*

bankruptcy crime An act committed in connection with a bankruptcy case that is punishable by a maximum of five years imprisonment, a maximum fine of $5,000, or both.

bankruptcy estate Any property belonging to a debtor at the time he files bankruptcy. It includes property in which the debtor has an interest, even if it is owned or held by another person.

bankruptcy mill A business other than a law firm that provides bankruptcy counseling and prepares bankruptcy petitions. *Also see typing service.*

bankruptcy petition A formal request for protection of the bankruptcy laws. There is an Official Form for bankruptcy petitions. *See sample in Appendix A.*

cc Originally, carbon copy; now, a photocopy. The notation *cc: Ms. Jones* placed on a document sent to Mr. Smith indicates to Mr. Smith that a copy of the document is also being sent to Ms. Jones.

Chapter 7 The portion of the Bankruptcy Code (11 U.S.C. §§ 701 - 766) providing for "liquidation"—distribution of a debtor's nonexempt property to his creditors.

Chapter 7 trustee A person appointed in a Chapter 7 case to represent the interests of the bankruptcy estate and the unsecured creditors. The trustee's responsibilities include reviewing the debtor's petition and schedules and distributing property of the bankruptcy estate to creditors. The trustee may also bring actions against creditors (or the debtor) to recover property of the bankruptcy estate.

Chapter 11 Business reorganization bankruptcy (11 U.S.C. §§ 1101 - 1174). A Chapter 11 debtor forms a plan of reorganization to keep its business alive and pay creditors over time. People in business or people who have assets greater than the debt limits set for Chapter 13 cases can seek relief in Chapter 11.

Chapter 12 Family farmer bankruptcy (11 U.S.C. §§ 1201 - 1231).

Chapter 13 Wage earner bankruptcy. The portion of the Bankruptcy Code (11 U.S.C. §§ 1301 - 1330) allowing a debtor to keep property and pay debts over time.

Chapter 13 trustee A person appointed to oversee administration of a Chapter 13 case. A Chapter 13 trustee's responsibilities are the same as those of a Chapter 7 trustee; however, a Chapter 13 trustee has the additional responsibilities of overseeing the debtor's plan and distributing plan payments to creditors.

claim The right of a creditor to money or other payment from a debtor or his property.

confirmation Approval of a Chapter 13 plan by a bankruptcy judge.

consumer bankruptcy A bankruptcy case filed to eliminate consumer debts.

consumer debts Debts incurred for personal (not business) needs.

contingent claim A claim is contingent if it is not certain that the debtor owes the creditor anything, but might owe him something.

cure To pay money that is past due under a contract or lease.

debtor A person who has filed a petition for protection of the federal bankruptcy laws.

discharge A release for a debtor from dischargeable debts. A discharge releases a debtor from personal liability for discharged debts and prevents the creditors owed those debts from taking any action against the debtor or his property to collect the debts. The discharge also prohibits creditors from making any communication regarding the debt with the debtor, his relatives, employees, or friends, including telephone calls, letters and personal contact; and from taking any action against the debtor's property to collect a discharged debt.

dischargeable debt A debt the Bankruptcy Code allows to be discharged.

equity The value of a debtor's interest in property that remains after creditors' interests are considered. Example: If you own a house valued at $90,000 and it is subject to a $50,000 mortgage, you have $40,000 equity in it.

executory contract or lease A contract or lease is "executory" if *both* parties to the agreement have duties to perform under it. If a contract or lease is executory, a debtor may assume (keep) it or reject (eliminate) it.

exempt A description of any property that a debtor may keep from creditors.

exemption Certain property the Bankruptcy Code or applicable state law permits a debtor to keep from creditors. The value of an exemption in specific property is deducted from the debtor's equity in the property, not from the total value of the property.

face sheet filing A bankruptcy case filed either without schedules or with schedules listing few creditors and debts. Face sheet filings are usually made for the purpose of delaying an eviction.

fraudulent transfer A transfer of a debtor's property for which he receives nothing or receives something worth less than the transferred property's value.

fresh start The characterization of a debtor's life after bankruptcy—free of burdensome debts. Giving debtors a fresh start is the fundamental purpose of the Bankruptcy Code.

insider A relative or business associate of a debtor.

involuntary transfer Transfer of a debtor's property without her consent. Example: If your wages were garnished, the garnishment is an involuntary transfer because you did not consent to it.

joint petition A husband and wife filing bankruptcy together with one bankruptcy petition.

lien A charge upon property securing a debt.

liquidation Disposal of a debtor's property for the benefit of his creditors.

liquidated claim A creditor's claim for a specific amount of money.

luxury goods or services Goods or services that are not basic necessities.

meeting of creditors *See 341 meeting.*

motion to lift the automatic stay A request by a creditor to allow him to take an action against a debtor or his property that is prohibited by the automatic stay.

no-asset case The typical Chapter 7 case where there are no assets available to satisfy creditors' unsecured claims.

nondischargeable debt A debt that cannot be discharged in bankruptcy.

objection to discharge A trustee's or creditor's objection to the debtor's discharge in general, or to the discharge of a specific debt.

objection to exemptions A trustee's or creditor's challenge of a debtor's attempt to exempt certain property.

petition *See bankruptcy petition.*

plan Under Chapter 13, a debtor's detailed description of how his creditors' claims will be paid over a period of time, usually three years.

postpetition transfer A transfer of a debtor's property made without permission from the bankruptcy court while the debtor's bankruptcy case is pending.

prebankruptcy planning Arrangement (or rearrangement) of a debtor's property to allow him to take maximum advantage of available exemptions. Prebankruptcy planning often includes converting nonexempt assets into exempt ones.

preferential debt payment A debt payment of more than $600 in the 90 days before a debtor files bankruptcy (or within one year if the creditor was a relative or business associate) that gives the creditor more money that she would receive in the debtor's Chapter 7 case.

priority Ranking of unsecured claims.

proof of claim A statement describing the reason a debtor owes a creditor money.

schedules Lists prepared by the debtor showing his assets, liabilities, and other financial information.

secured claim A debt for which property has been pledged to a creditor to insure payment. Example: a home mortgage.

state exemptions *See exemptions.*

substantial abuse The characterization of a bankruptcy case in which debtors file bankruptcy although they are able to pay their debts when due.

341 meeting A meeting at which the debtor appears before his creditors to be questioned about his financial affairs.

transfer Any means by which a debtor is separated from his property.

typing service A business other than a law firm that prepares bankruptcy petitions. *Also see bankruptcy mill.*

United States Trustee An officer of the Justice Department responsible for overseeing bankruptcy cases.

undersecured claim A debt secured by property worth less than the amount of the debt.

unlawful detainer A person against whom an *unlawful detainer action* has been brought.

unlawful detainer action A lawsuit brought by a landlord against his tenant to evict the tenant—usually for nonpayment of rent.

unliquidated claim A claim for which no specific value has been assigned.

unsecured claim A claim for which none of a debtor's property has been pledged.

voluntary transfer A transfer of a debtor's property by payment of a debt, a sale, giving a gift, or other means, with the debtor's consent.

Index

About the Author

Alice Griffin is a graduate of Wellesley College and the UCLA School of Law. During her clerkship with a United States Bankruptcy Judge she observed thousands of consumer bankruptcy cases. Through the Legal Aid Society and the Association of the Bar of the City of New York, Ms. Griffin gives free assistance to people filing bankruptcy.

Notes

Notes

Notes

Notes

Notes

Notes

THE CAKEWALK PRESS

ORDER FORM

I'd like to order *Personal Bankruptcy: What You Should Know* for $13.95 postpaid. Please send to:

Name _____

Address _____

City/State/Zip _____

Qty.	Title	Amount	Total
	Personal Bankruptcy: What You Should Know	$13.95	
	$1.15 NY sales tax for each book shipped to a NY address		
	GRAND TOTAL		

*Make check or money order payable
to **The Cakewalk Press** and mail it and this form to:*

The Cakewalk Press
P.O. Box 1536-B
New York, NY 10276